# THOROUGHBRED LEGENDS

# Dr. Fager

## RACING'S TOP RECORD SETTER

THOROUGHBRED LEGENDS

# Dr. Fager
## RACING'S TOP RECORD SETTER

BY STEVE HASKIN

ECLIPSE
PRESS

Lexington, Kentucky

Library of Congress Card Number: 99-68805

ISBN-13: 978-1-58150-175-9 (trade paperback)
ISBN-10: 1-58150-175-7 (trade paperback)
Originally published in hardcover, 2000

Printed in the United States

a division of
Blood-Horse Publications
PUBLISHERS SINCE 1916

# Contents

# INTRODUCTION

# ...Farewell To All My Greatness!

from, *Henry VIII*, by Shakespeare

November 14, 1968, looked like any other late autumn morning on the Belmont Park backstretch. The stinging winds blowing in off Jamaica Bay made trainers and barn workers thankful the annual mass exodus of man and beast to Florida was only weeks away.

But this was not any other morning. Across the road from the track kitchen, the familiar glow that had emanated from Barn 41 for the past three years was rapidly dimming. In a few moments it would be gone forever, taking with it a fire and spirit never before seen on an American racetrack. Maybe that's what made this morning seem a little bit colder than usual.

Outside the barn, Tartan Stable's green and white private van awaited its illustrious passenger. Soon, it would roll out the stable gate onto

Hempstead Turnpike, beginning its journey to Tartan Farm in Ocala, Florida, where Dr. Fager would begin his new life as a stallion. As the moment of departure neared, the atmosphere at the barn grew solemn. One by one, barn workers went up to Dr. Fager's stall to say their goodbyes. Groom and swing man Freddy (Beetle) Dimitrijevic, sixteen-year-old son of assistant trainer Spasoje (Joe) Dimitrijevic, walked up to the Doc and stroked him on the forehead. "Have a good trip," he said. "I hope to see you again soon."

At 8 o'clock, Dr. Fager was ready for the 30-hour trip back to his place of birth. His groom, Joe (Pack Rat) Findley, had fed the colt a light breakfast of oats and bran and mineral oil an hour earlier. A half-dozen jugs of Mountain Valley mineral water from Hot Springs, Arkansas, were then loaded on the van.

Earlier that morning, Dr. Fager had gone out for his final gallop with exercise rider Henry Skaates aboard. Jose Marrero, the colt's regular rider for the past two years, was suffering from a bad back and asked Skaates if he'd like to gallop him that morning. "He felt as strong as he ever did," said Skaates, who had galloped Dr. Fager on several occasions. He took a firm hold on him, knowing full well you didn't want to move your hands on this horse, especially on his final morning at the track.

At 8:25, trainer John Nerud attached the shank to Dr. Fager's halter and led the big bay out of the barn for the last time. Outside, bundled up in heavy jackets and overcoats, barn workers lined up for one final look at the great Dr. Fager. One of them held up a sign which simply read, "Farewell, Doc!"

As the horse emerged from the barn and strode majestically into the chilling November air, a gust of wind blew his long mane on end, giving it a plume-like effect, as if atop the head of a Trojan warrior. Dr. Fager arched his neck and flared his nostrils just as he had done so many times in battle. Once the horse was on the van, Nerud tossed in a bale of alfalfa. He went over to the colt, gave him a pat on the nose and said, "See you in Florida, old boy."

Then the van drove off, leaving nothing behind but silence and memories. Nerud went back in the barn and looked in Stall 4, which had been Dr. Fager's home for nearly three years. "Boys," he said, "this is the emptiest stall I've ever seen."

"We all felt like we had lost something," Freddy Dimitrijevic said. "The spirit just wasn't the same, and it took quite a while to build it back up."

The following afternoon, as the van neared its destination, it was stopped by Marion County Deputy Sheriff Don Moreland, who welcomed the arrival of Dr. Fager with his own brand of Southern hospitality. Accompanied by a photographer to record the historic moment, Moreland, a husky chap with hair cropped close to his scalp, stepped inside the van. He walked up to a curious Dr. Fager and presented him with a summons. Written on the ticket were two words: "Reckless speed."

Meanwhile, back at Belmont, Nerud decided to leave the webbing up on Dr. Fager's stall and keep everything just as it was. It would be a long time before he would put another horse in there. Looking at the webbing, Nerud and Dimitrijevic couldn't help but think back to the mischievous two-year-old who had arrived at the barn at Hialeah in the winter of 1966. Nerud's barn was right near the entrance to the pad-dock. Every afternoon, the youngster would lie down in his stall and stick his head under the webbing until it was well out in the shed row. When he got up, he was so strong, he'd rip the webbing right out of the wall. Sometimes, he'd just crawl under it. Once free from the confines of his stall, he would dash out of the barn and head to the paddock, where he'd frolic about until someone came and got him. Before long, Dr. Fager's daily escape to the paddock became a routine occurrence.

It was as if he knew that this was to be the arena where he would one day prepare himself for battle. This was where the fire would start to build; where he would take the weight off his leg ever so slightly, and the muscles in his shoulder would begin to quiver. Whenever Nerud saw that look, he knew the Doc was ready to rip the pages out of the history books. By the time the colt had reached the starting gate, his eyes were as big as saucers. As he'd lift his head, his entire body — all sixteen hands, two inches of it — seemed to expand, like a blowfish swelling to twice its size. Horses who were of equal height just minutes earlier, now appeared dwarfed by him.

Although Dr. Fager was a flash of lightning as a two-year-old and three-year-old, the thunder would not come until he was four. That's when Nerud put a figure-eight bridle on the colt, let his mane and foretop grow long, then turned him loose. It was if he had released a wild mustang from captivity. Now bigger and stronger, and no match for any mere mortal on his back, Dr. Fager finally was free to romp with reckless abandon. And did he love it.

What followed was a campaign many believe to be the greatest in the history of the sport. It would end with an unprecedented four championships — Horse of the Year, Handicap Horse, Sprinter, and Turf Horse, a feat not likely to be duplicated.

Dr. Fager laughed in the faces of racing secretaries, who could find no weight burdensome enough to stop him. They piled as much as 139 pounds on his back, but all that broke were stopwatches and teletimers. He left two track records — seven furlongs in 1:20 1/5 under 139 pounds and a world-record mile in 1:32 1/5 under 134 pounds — burnt deep in the sandy loam of Aqueduct and Arlington Park. There they would remain for thirty-one years and twenty-nine years, respectively.

Dr. Fager also equaled the track record for a mile and a quarter at Aqueduct, defeating his arch rival Damascus in 1:59 3/5, carrying 132 pounds, a little over a month after almost dying from colic. In his only start on grass, the United Nations Handicap, he lost the lead three times on a slick course he detested, but came back each time, despite carrying 134 pounds, to defeat a star-studded field of grass specialists. The previous year, he had set two track records at Rockingham Park and run the fastest mile by a three-year-old in the history of New York racing.

But statistics, mind-boggling as they were, are only a part of the Dr. Fager legacy. With his long mane blowing wildly in the breeze and the fire burning in his eyes, he was a force of unharnessed energy. It was as if he had leaped off the pages of a children's novel. Here before our eyes was the Black Stallion dressed in a brown coat with black trimmings. His color seemed to change with the light, turning from a rich blood bay to a burnished copper. All he wanted in front of him was the wind blowing in his face, and if another horse dared to disturb that scene, the Doc made him pay dearly. Even the fastest of the fast crumbled when Dr. Fager looked him in the eye. Once, when another of his arch rivals, In Reality, foolishly tried to sneak up on his inside, the good doctor reached over and savaged him.

It was memories such as these that swirled through the November winds that morning on the Belmont backstretch. And it was only fitting that the last image people saw of Dr. Fager as he pranced out of his barn for the final time was of that same wild, tempestuous colt, the likes of whom we shall never see again.

*Steve Haskin*
*Hamilton Square, New Jersey*
*December 1999*

# Long Legs And Winged Feet

The morning of April 6, 1964, seemed just like any other to nineteen-year-old Al Roberts, who was starting his third year as a groom in the foaling barn at Tartan Farm. He had no way of knowing it, but a very special friend was about to enter his life. In a few hours a gangly-legged foal by Rough'n Tumble out of Aspidistra would be born, and the two would embark on a thirteen-year journey, during which both would learn about trust and the bond that has existed for centuries between man and horse. They were together at birth and would be together at death, teaching each other valuable lessons along the way.

Like the vast majority of broodmares, Aspidistra was expected to give birth at night or in the pre-dawn hours. But the foal kicking inside her was not an ordinary foal. All through his life, he would do things his way, and that included being born. This wouldn't be the first time he would defy the clock or put time in a different perspective.

As the hours rolled by and afternoon approached, the chances of Aspidistra's having her foal grew slim. Mares normally just don't give birth in the middle of the day. Roberts had been watching her closely and was told to put her in a small paddock and monitor her from there. He wasn't expecting much to happen at that hour, but soon after being brought out, Aspidistra began showing the first signs of labor. Then her water broke. Roberts called farm manager John Hartigan. By the time he arrived at the foaling barn, Aspidistra was back in the stall and preparing to have her foal.

Everything went smoothly, and at 12:55 p.m. she delivered a strapping bay colt. The first thing everyone noticed was how extraordinarily long this little guy's legs were...much more so than an average foal's. Because of that, it took the colt precisely forty-five minutes finally to get to his feet. At 2:10, thirty minutes after taking his first steps, he began nursing.

He was a strong, healthy foal, but with his long back, narrow chest, and long legs, Hartigan felt he would grow to be too skinny and gangly. He also had two club feet, a deformity of the joint in the coffin bone. Nerud knew right away he was not salable, although he had no intention of selling anyway. "He wouldn't have brought five thousand dollars," Nerud said.

Roberts could see immediately this was no ordinary foal. At Tartan, foals were taught to lead the day after being born. Normally, as they were led out to their paddock, there would be one person holding the mare and one holding the foal. But Aspidistra's colt was so easy-going, and learned so quickly, only one person was needed to handle both mare and foal. At Tartan, there was an old plum tree in front of the barn, and after three days, as Roberts approached the tree with Aspidistra and her foal, he'd turn loose the foal, who would walk around the tree by himself and meet up with his mother on the other side.

The following year, after being weaned, the colt headed to the yearling barn to be broken. Roberts was transferred there and continued his relationship with the colt, who was now beginning to grow into his long legs and develop into a powerhouse. Also in that crop of yearlings were an Intentionally colt, owned by

Frances Genter, later to be named In Reality, and two other promising Rough'n Tumble colts, later named Minnesota Mac and Ruffled Feathers.

When it was time to be broken, Aspidistra's son and a still-green Roberts both learned by teaching each other. Tartan used the European method of lunging and driving to break the yearlings. One by one, new equipment was added. Roberts introduced a key bit to the colt's mouth and placed a pair of boots on his ankles to keep them from hitting each other. The youngster quickly grabbed hold of the foreign object in his mouth, which was equipped with small keys protruding from the middle to allow him to work up saliva and keep his mouth moist, while acting as a pacifier. In the future, however, bits would come to represent restraint and that would go against the colt's nature.

The more Nerud saw of the colt, the more he liked him. He was big and rugged, with tremendous leverage. He also had the kind of long hip that Nerud equated with power. He still was kind of clumsy with those long legs, and when he went to the track for his morning gallops, he would stumble, nearly tripping over himself. But once he got his legs going in unison, he no longer felt awkward and tentative. As he began reaching out with new-found confidence, his stride grew longer and more fluid. Soon he was taking two strides to every three by the other yearlings.

He was beginning to look more and more like a big brute, but in truth he was a very sensitive horse who didn't liked to be scolded, hit, or yelled at. "Even as a stallion, if you scolded him, you actually would hurt his feelings," Roberts said. As a racehorse, he would come to detest the whip. He always gave his all, and on the rare occasions he did feel the sting of the whip, he'd throw his tail straight up in the air in defiance.

Although he grew into a towering inferno on the racetrack, the flame that drove him would quickly extinguish once he was back in the barn among friends. Replacing it was a gentle glow that lit up everyone around him. As a stallion, he once took on the role of nursemaid and protector to a litter of kittens who were born in his stall. Each day after coming in from his paddock, as soon as his halter was removed, he would walk over to check on the kittens, bending down and giving them a slight nuzzle before heading to his feed tub. When the mother cat finally removed the kittens from the stall, he appeared noticeably upset.

As the yearling colt continued to progress at the farm in the spring of 1965, tragedy struck a thousand miles away in New York. It happened quickly and unexpectedly, and came within a heartbeat of changing the face of racing in this country. Nerud, the heart and soul of Tartan Farm, not to mention a twenty-five percent owner in the operation, was on his pony when one of the stable's cheaper horses ran off with his "drunken" rider. Nerud decided to go after the horse, a decision that nearly cost him his life. As he was nearing the runaway animal, Nerud reached over to him when his pony suddenly lurched, throwing Nerud head over heels. He landed heavily on his head, but shrugged it off and continued as if nothing had happened.

For the next thirty-six days, Nerud was like a zombie, unaware that a massive blood clot was forming on his brain. Although he would pass out occasionally, he still kept going. But when he returned from a Nebraska hunting trip, his wife Charlotte saw right away something was dreadfully wrong. A Boston native, she was familiar with the famed Lahey Clinic, and soon, she and her husband were on a plane bound for her hometown. They checked into a hotel near the hospital, but at first were refused a room, because the clerk thought Nerud was drunk.

Once at the clinic, Nerud was examined by the head of neurosurgery, Dr. Charles Fager. He took one look in Nerud's eyes and scheduled surgery. "He was on death's door and didn't know it," Fager said.

The surgery to remove the blood clot and alleviate the severe swelling in the brain succeeded. But a short time later, while in a hotel room, Nerud began suffering from spasms. Fager performed another operation and told Nerud there was nothing else he could do for him.

While recuperating, Nerud had to attend to the business of naming that year's crop of yearlings. Of the Rough'n Tumbles, one was out of the good mare Cow Girl, who had already produced a good horse for Tartan. Because William McKnight, owner of Tartan, was from Minnesota and his company was located in Minnesota, Nerud wanted to name one of the better horses Minnesota Mac. "He liked that old mare," Nerud recalled. "If her colt turned out to be the better of the two, he would have been real disappointed."

So Nerud chose the name Minnesota Mac for the Cow Girl colt. Then it was time to name Aspidistra's son. Sitting in his wheelchair outside his room, still attached to an intravenous unit, Nerud wrote a note of authorization, giving him permission to name a horse for the man who saved his life. As Dr. Fager walked by, Nerud handed him the note and told him to sign it. Because of his condition, the handwriting was barely legible. Fager took the note, gave it a quick glance, then hurriedly scribbled his signature, thinking nothing of it. Little did he know that as he was signing his name to that insignificant note he was also immortalizing it.

For Nerud, the big, powerful bay who was learning his lessons so well at Tartan Farm couldn't have come along at a more opportune time. Politics were at work at the upper level of the McKnight organization. After Nerud's accident and surgery, several people close to McKnight tried to convince him that his trainer and partner in Tartan Stable was suffering from brain cancer.

But those rumors and innuendoes were silenced the following year when Nerud unleashed the Tartan titan known as Dr. Fager. "Like out of nowhere," Nerud said, "here came this great big red ball of fire emerging from the horizon like the sunrise. Just like that, I was miraculously cured."

# "Mr. Nerud, you may execute your plan."

John Nerud was born in 1913 in the small town of Minatare, in the northwest corner of Nebraska, just about two miles from the North Platte River. One of nine children, Nerud grew up in a log cabin, "just like Lincoln." Instead of floors, he walked on dirt. The winters were hard and cold, and it was an unpleasant chore bringing the cattle in from pasture. As Nerud put it, all they had to break the bone-chilling wind that howled down from the Rocky Mountains was a barbed wire fence.

"When school started, we were the happiest damn kids in the world," he said. School consisted of two rooms: One for grades one through six, and the other for grades seven through twelve.

The family couldn't afford to hire help, so Nerud was forced to learn how to handle horses at an early age. He was a full-fledged cowboy at the age of five, and could handle a team of horses in the field by age six.

Young Nerud was a rogue who learned how to live by his wits. "I was full of hell all the time," he said. He wouldn't change much in the next eighty years.

In order to make some money on his own, he started out riding in rodeos while in high school, but after being thrown more often than not, he decided it would be safer and more profitable at the racetrack. He wasn't any more proficient at riding Thoroughbreds, so that quickly ended any thoughts of becoming a jockey. Riding in Nerud's neck of the woods meant relay races, "similar to the Pony Express," in which the rider would dismount and change saddles every half-mile.

Nerud began looking for horses to buy. He and his brother would go to the local auctions and buy cheap horses who were selling "under the halter," meaning there was something wrong with them.

On one occasion he purchased a draft mare for seventeen dollars who was selling "as you see her." That was pretty steep compared to the five dollars he'd pay for some of them. After getting her home, Nerud discovered that every time he'd drive her, she'd go backward instead of forward. He cured her of that habit, and eventually traded her to a passerby who was looking for a good draft horse. The horse he got in return was a four-year-old Thoroughbred named Dr. Coogle, who was a bit of a rogue himself. Nerud worked with him and won several races with him at the bush tracks in Harrison and Mitchell, Nebraska, before losing him in a claiming race the following year. Dr. Coogle would go on to race through his seventeenth year, developing into a "damn good horse," as Nerud recalled. "I had no idea what I had," he said. "Otherwise, I wouldn't have put him in a claiming race. When you're young you're dumb."

At a typical race meet in Eastern Nebraska, local cowboys were hired to serves as judges, or stewards, and they would stand atop a platform in the infield. The best rider around at the time was Johnny Adams, who would go on to greater fame as both a jockey and the trainer of the brilliant J. O. Tobin. Because of his success at the bush tracks, many of the other riders accused him of using a battery. When they complained to the judge, he asked, "Well, what does a battery do?" and they would reply, "It makes the horse run faster." The judge looked back quizzically and said, "So, what's the problem? All of you get one."

Perhaps one of the reasons Nerud has always been able to handle owners and stand firmly by his principles was his association with Sid Williams of Harrison, Nebraska. After Williams, all owners must have seemed tame to Nerud. Williams, known as "Bring 'Em Back Alive" Sid, was sheriff of Sioux County and had four horses that he wanted the young Nerud to train. Williams, who was seventy when he hooked up with the twenty-year-old Nerud, had known many of the West's old gunslingers, and as sheriff had to deal mostly with horse and cattle rustlers and bootleggers. Even at seventy, Williams would wear a pair of pearl-handled pistols, hung low on his hips with the holster straps tied around his leg.

"He wore those pistols every damn minute of his life," Nerud said. "I think he slept in them. Back in the early days, the local sheriffs would run the bootleggers and rustlers off, but they always came back. So, they got Sid to bring them in. He'd just walk up to them and said, 'Come.' If they didn't he killed them. He was the goddamn law back then and he wasn't afraid to do it."

Nerud trained for Williams in Rapid City and Hot Springs, South Dakota, before leaving and taking on a string of horses in Montana. He soon began buying his own horses, including a classy colt named Air Chute.

His travels then took him to Havana, Cuba, where he admittedly did mostly nothing. He eventually became agent for jockey Ted Atkinson. He hustled mounts for Atkinson while buying horses for himself before leaving to serve in the Navy during World War II, where he saw action in the South Pacific. When he returned, he had enough money to start buying better horses. He went to Florida "to finally start living like a human being," and became assistant to Woolford Farm trainer Frank Kearns, who had trained Bull Lea. He did well with the horses entrusted to him, and Woolford Farm owner Herbert Woolf took a liking to him, eventually naming Nerud as trainer. In 1949, he trained Delegate, who was voted co-champion sprinter of that year.

As the good horses came, so did the owners. One of them was Ralph Lowe, an oil tycoon from Midland, Texas. In 1955, Humphrey Finney, president of the Fasig-Tipton Sales Company, purchased several yearlings from the Aga Khan on behalf of Lowe. The following year, Lowe turned the horses over to Nerud to train. Among them was a smallish son of Migoli named Gallant Man. The colt wasn't an exceptional individual physically, but would prove to be one of the outstanding stayers of his time.

In 1957, the forty-four-year-old Nerud, his dues paid, burst into the national spotlight under the Twin Spires of Churchill Downs. But it was not victory that awaited him on that cold and windy first Saturday in May. Instead, he entered Derby folklore through one of the most bizarre occurrences in the history of the race.

Gallant Man went into the eighty-third Kentucky Derby as the 7-2 co-second choice, coming off a nose defeat to the Derby favorite Bold Ruler in the Wood Memorial. Several nights before the race, Lowe dreamed that Gallant Man was on his way to certain victory when his rider misjudged the finish line and stood up in the irons before the wire, costing Gallant Man the victory. At the time,

Lowe was insistent about using Bill Shoemaker, while Nerud preferred Johnny Choquette, who had ridden the horse in the majority of his races. The debate was settled when Choquette was handed a ten-day suspension.

At the Brown Hotel the night before the race, Nerud and Lowe had a good laugh about the dream. Nerud assured him, "Ralph, you'll sleep better tonight. You've got your jock and he won't pull him up."

Coming down the stretch, Gallant Man was charging at the leader, Iron Liege, when Shoemaker, who had already ridden in five Kentucky Derbys, winning on Swaps in 1955, stood up in the irons just as he was about to pass Iron Liege. He quickly realized his mistake, but it was too late. Iron Liege held on to win by a nose.

Lowe just stood there in shock. The innocent dream he and Nerud had laughed about was now as real as Iron Liege's number lighting up the tote board. A furious Nerud rushed down to the track to confront Shoemaker. All he wanted was for the rider to admit his mistake and not blame the horse. "If he'd said something about the horse, I was gonna hit him with the f—-in' (field) glasses,"

Nerud was quoted as saying. But as soon as Shoemaker saw Nerud, he said, "I'm sorry, John. I made a mistake." The incident was over.

Nerud went against the book and decided to skip the Preakness, pointing Gallant Man instead for the Belmont Stakes. People tried to convince him to head to Baltimore, but, not knowing Nerud, they weren't aware that they were attempting to break through an impenetrable wall. Gallant Man romped by eight lengths in the Belmont, setting a track and American record that would not be broken until Secretariat shattered it sixteen years later. He confirmed his reputation as the top stayer in America later that year by winning the Travers Stakes and two-mile Jockey Club Gold Cup.

That same year, Everett Clay, publicity director at Hialeah, told Nerud that William McKnight, chairman of the board and major stockholder of Minnesota Mining and Manufacturing (3-M), was looking for a trainer. McKnight, who had recently made Florida his winter residence, had become interested in racing after visiting Hialeah for the first time. Because of his Scottish heritage, he adorned his red silks with a tartan-like sash and named his stable after the familiar garb of the Scottish Highlands. When one of McKnight's scientists at 3-M invented an adhesive applied to the back of long, sturdy stripping, McKnight named the new product Scotch Tape.

Clay, who also was secretary of the Florida Thoroughbred Breeders' Association, had done work for McKnight, and knew that his interest in racing was long-term. McKnight wanted to enjoy all that the sport had to offer, while building another empire along the way. Clay immediately thought of Nerud as the man to help him achieve both.

When Clay told Nerud about McKnight, the trainer responded in typical fashion. "Hell, there ain't nobody from Minnesota that has any money," Nerud said. "I've already got Lowe and (Joseph) Roebling. Now, they're rich."

Nerud then called Lowe and told him about the offer, and asked him what he knew about McKnight. An hour later, Lowe called Nerud back and said, "John, now you're talking about big money. You think Roebling and I have money? This guy is rich."

McKnight, a native of Wheat, South Dakota, was already listed by *Fortune* magazine as one of the wealthiest men in America. By 1968, his wealth would be estimated at between $300 million and $500 million. Like a shark smelling blood, Nerud immediately called Clay and told him to set up an appointment with McKnight.

Nerud, well aware of his own abilities, knew what McKnight was looking for, and he was determined to tell him how to go about achieving it. That was the only way Nerud knew how to do things. Like old Sid Williams, he always shot from the hip and rarely missed his target.

The first thing Nerud told McKnight was that he needed a hobby, but it would not come cheap. "I already have a hobby," McKnight responded. When Nerud asked him what it was, he replied, "Making money." Nerud assured him the payoff of this new hobby would be the enjoyment and the sportsmanship McKnight was seeking. When McKnight questioned him on how he was planning to achieve that, Nerud said bluntly, "First off, you give me a million dollars. If that doesn't work, you give me two million dollars. If that doesn't work, you give me three million dollars." According to Nerud, that's when McKnight's lawyer, accountant, and partner in the outdoor advertising business, who were sitting in on the meeting, nearly fell out of their chairs.

Nerud told McKnight there wasn't anyone in the business who knew how to buy yearlings, so he'd have to set up a factory-like operation — starting with a farm, then building up a broodmare band and breeding their own horses. McKnight told Nerud to put it all in a letter, and he'd think about it. Nerud complied, but didn't hear back from McKnight for a while. He finally received a letter, saying simply, "Dear Mr. Nerud, you may execute your plan."

"I didn't know it," Nerud said, "but he had his accountants and lawyers talking to every racing secretary they could find about me. He had actually compiled a dossier on me."

McKnight had a few cheap horses in training at the time. After a while, he contacted Nerud, asking why there wasn't much action. Nerud answered, "We don't have anything to get action with. Give me a hundred thousand grand to put in the claiming box and I'll get you action." McKnight obliged, and when that money was spent, Nerud asked for another hundred grand. Nerud claimed several good horses, and the victories soon began piling up. So, McKnight now had the action he was looking for, and at the same time was beginning to build his new hobby into one of the most successful breeding operations in the country.

Unbeknownst to McKnight and Nerud, an incident took place in September of 1957 that would have a profound effect, not only on the emergence of Tartan Stable as a dominant force, but on the Sport of Kings itself.

For his seventieth birthday, McKnight's executive staff decided to do something special. They collected $6,500 among themselves and handed it over to trainer John Sceusa, who had two horses at the time for McKnight. They told Sceusa to look for a horse they could buy as a birthday gift for their boss.

Sceusa wound up using the money to purchase the three-year-old filly Aspidistra. To this day, no one knows why. "The filly couldn't run," Nerud said. "I don't know why he picked her, but he did."

Plagued by bad knees, the daughter of Better Self out of Tilly Rose did not win a race in three tries for McKnight and retired at the end of 1957 with two victories in fourteen career starts for meager earnings of $5,115. If there was one thing she was not known for during her one-year career, it was speed. Her two six-furlong victories, both at Fair Grounds, were accomplished in a pedestrian 1:14 3/5 and 1:14 4/5. There was no way anyone could have dreamed her son and daughter would win four consecutive sprint championships between them.

The purchase of Aspidistra is riddled with inconsistencies, and although it has been reported through the years that she had been claimed by Sceusa, there is no record of it in the *Daily Racing Form*. When she ran for the first time ever for a claiming tag on September 25, 1957, she was already owned by Tartan. In her previous start, twelve days earlier, she raced for owner M. Preston. Even the purchase price of $6,500 is open to question, considering that she did run in a claiming race at Hawthorne for the exact same price in her first start for Tartan, not something one normally would do with a newly received birthday present. In any event, it would turn out to be one of the great purchases in the history of the sport.

It also would be the last Tartan transaction not orchestrated by Nerud, who eventually became a twenty-five percent partner and ran the operation with an iron fist. McKnight wanted his breeding operation in Florida, so Nerud purchased 320 acres in Ocala from Bonnie Heath, and did all the price negotiating. According to Heath, he received a thousand dollars an acre. Ocala at the time consisted of fewer than one hundred breeding farms, the majority of which were small, family-run operations with only a handful of broodmares.

Nerud knew that 320 acres would not be sufficient for his grandiose plans, so he acquired an additional 700 acres across the street. Among the first horses to arrive at the farm were a group of mares that had been purchased in a package deal by McKnight from Garden State Park and Hialeah owner Eugene Mori and the recently retired Aspidistra. According to Nerud, Aspidistra, after being retired, had been sent to a guy in Ocala who "went to jail for killing somebody over a broad." He bred her to an obscure stallion named Esmero and she produced a filly named Perplexing, who would go on to win four races. When Nerud got her, he bred her to First Cabin and got stakes-winning A. Deck. He then bred her to Needles, and the result was Chinatowner, winner of the Canadian Turf Handicap at Gulfstream Park.

One of Nerud's initial goals was to obtain a young horse that had the potential to become a top-class sire. While at Belmont Park one afternoon, an agent suggested that Nerud go to the paddock and look at this one horse. His name was Intentionally, and not only was he an attractive individual, he was one of the fastest horses on the grounds and traced to the Man o' War sire line. Nerud took an immediate liking to the horse and asked his owner, Harry Isaacs, how much he wanted for him. When Isaacs said $750,000, Nerud agreed. All he had to do now was call McKnight and tell him that he just bought him a horse for $750,000. Considering he had never paid more than $20,000 of McKnight's money for any one horse, it was going to be an interesting conversation.

The news brought nothing but silence on the other end. Nerud, taking advantage of the situation, jumped in and told McKnight where to transfer the money. When McKnight said okay, Nerud knew he now had total control of Tartan

Farm and a free rein to build it up in whatever manner he chose. The mating of Aspidistra to Intentionally in 1965 would produce two-time champion sprinter Ta Wee, who pioneered new ground in weight carrying. In addition to winning the Vosburgh Handicap, she closed out her career with victories in the Fall Highweight and Interborough Handicaps, carrying 140 and 142 pounds, respectively.

After retiring Intentionally and breeding the majority of the Tartan mares to the young stallion, Nerud realized if the horse turned out to be a bust, he would have a hard time explaining it. So, he began looking for another stallion. In the early 1960s, Joe O'Farrell, one of Florida's most noted horsemen, was conducting a tent sale, selling a number of broodmares in foal to the twelve-year-old stallion Rough'n Tumble, who was hampered by a plastic foot, which made it hard for him to breed. When several of the mares sold for prices ranging from $300 to $800, Fasig-Tipton's Humphrey Finney stopped the sale and told O'Farrell he was giving these horses away. He suggested O'Farrell bring over his Rough'n Tumble foals and show everyone how good they looked.

O'Farrell did as Humphrey suggested. One person who was extremely impressed by the foals was Nerud, who had already purchased a share in Rough'n Tumble from O'Farrell for $25,000. He respected O'Farrell and liked the horse's pedigree. But now with a plastic foot, the stallion's popularity had plummeted. The first thing Nerud did was contact Bonnie Heath and offer to purchase his season in Rough'n Tumble. Heath said a season was $5,000 and he'd sell Nerud his share for the same price. All Nerud said was, "I'll take it." A few days later, Nerud received a call from an owner who had heard he was buying shares in Rough'n Tumble. He offered him his share for $7,500. "I'll take it," Nerud said. Soon after, he was contacted by someone offering to sell him his share in the stallion for $10,000. "I'll take it," Nerud said. Then it was Ralph Wilson who called Nerud from Buffalo, New York.

"If you're looking for Rough'n Tumble shares I've got one for sale," Wilson said.

"How much?" Nerud answered.

"I'll sell it to you for $12,500," Wilson said.

"I'll take it," Nerud replied.

When Wilson asked about insurance terms,

Nerud shot back, "Ralph, you want to sell the share? I'll mail you the check and you sell me the goddamn share. That's all there is to it."

With the share Nerud already had in Rough'n Tumble, that gave him five altogether. From those five shares came the 1964 foals Dr. Fager; Ruffled Feathers, who would go on to win the Man o' War Stakes; and the stakes-winning Minnesota Mac.

"Everyone in Ocala was snickering when I bought up all those shares," Nerud said. "It was like, 'We got a new sucker in town.' After buying the shares, I went to Joe O'Farrell's farm, where Rough'n Tumble was standing, and I asked the farm manager how the horse was doing. He said, 'It's hard for him to get up on the mares, because when he comes down it kind of hurts his foot. But he'll breed 'em.' I told him, 'That's okay, I just need one year out of him.'"

And what a year it was. In April, 1964, Rough'n Tumble's son out of Aspidistra was born. No one would ever snicker at John Nerud again.

# The Flame Is Ignited

John Nerud was convinced he had something. He wasn't quite sure just what, but all he knew was that it was worth showing off. It was the winter of 1966, and most of the big outfits were settled in their barns at Hialeah.

Willard Proctor, one of the deans of the Southern California circuit, was at Hialeah, and when Nerud spotted his old friend, he called him over to the barn.

"Willard, come on over here, I want to show you a good horse," Nerud said.

Nerud had the two-year-old Dr. Fager brought out and displayed him like a recently discovered work of art.

"Well, he is an impressive horse," the taciturn Proctor said.

Nerud told him he was an unraced two-year-old who was remarkably intelligent, especially for a young horse. Nerud was well aware of Dr. Fager's afternoon excursions to the paddock. When a young horse is this clever and resourceful, it's best to let him know who's boss before he starts doing everything his own way. Joe Dimitrijevic, who ran Nerud's stable for so many years, figured out a way to cure the Doc of his little habit. "He's a smart guy," Dimitrijevic said. "I'm gonna fix him." Whenever the horse would lie down and stick his head under the webbing, Dimitrijevic would walk up behind him with a broom and give him a gentle smack over the nose. "He pulled that head in damn quick," Nerud said. "If he stuck it out again, Joe would snap him back on the nose." Before long, the Doc was cured of that habit. But the racetrack was a different story. That would become Dr. Fager's domain, and once the gates opened, there wasn't a human on Earth who could tell him what to do.

But in the early days, when the fire was still in its infancy, Dr. Fager was a willing student and did whatever he was asked. If you wanted him to go fast, he'd go fast. If you wanted him to go slow, he'd go slow. If Nerud and Dimitrijevic wanted the Doc to run along with horses, he obliged. If they wanted him to bury them, he was gone. As the horse's training regimen increased, so did Nerud's confidence.

Nerud never believed in working horses fast. His philosophy, which was passed on to him by the great Ben Jones, was simple: "You don't get paid to work; you get paid to run." When the young Nerud took over the Woolford Farm horses, Jones, who had trained Kentucky Derby winner Lawrin for Woolf, came over to him and gave him words of wisdom Nerud always lived by. "Now son, listen to me," Jones said. "You ain't got enough sense to train these horses, so I'm gonna tell you what to do. You keep 'em fat, work 'em a half-mile, and they'll win in spite of you." He rode off and didn't say another word about it.

Nerud adopted Jones' philosophy, and he soon became a source of frustration for the clockers and bettors. Whenever someone would come up to *Daily Racing Form* clocker Eugene (Frenchy) Schwartz in New York and ask him what he thought about one of Nerud's horses, he'd say, "How the hell would I know? That half-mile sonofabitch, you don't know anything about him." Soon, Nerud became known in New York as that "half-mile sonofabitch."

So, when Nerud brought the Tartan horses up to New York from Florida in the spring of 1966, no one knew anything about his big, powerful bay colt named Dr. Fager or Nerud's other top prospect, Minnesota Mac. All Nerud knew was that he had never been around a horse who did things as effortlessly as Dr. Fager. He could either put him behind horses or send him to the lead. Either way, Dr. Fager, as Nerud put it, "would come down the stretch laughing, with his ears pricked." It didn't take long for his exercise rider, Jose Marrero, to realize he was on something special. He would get off the big bay and proclaim to whoever was listening, "This horse is a runner."

Among the key members of the Tartan team besides Marrero was Dr. Fager's groom Joe Findley, whom Nerud called "Pack Rat," because of his habit of taking anything he could get his hands on. When Nerud sent Dr. Fager to Arlington Park the following year, he was provided with a set of lounge chairs by the track. As they were leaving, Nerud noticed Findley loading the chairs on the van. At Saratoga, he often was seen at the nearby dump, rummaging for whatever he could find.

Marrero, whom Nerud estimated weighed 165 pounds under tack, had been around for years and acquired a good deal of racetrack savvy. "We used to send Dr. Fager out with a pony," Nerud said, "and when Jose would get to a certain spot, he'd tell the pony rider, 'Stop right here.' He'd raise up in the stirrups and survey the entire track to see if there was something that didn't look right."

Assistant trainer Spasoje (Joe) Dimitrijevic was the glue that held the barn together. It was Dimitrijevic's son, Fred, who introduced his father to Nerud. Fred was nicknamed "Beetle," after the Beatles because of his long hair and "mod" clothes. His father had been a trainer and jockey in his native Yugoslavia, and had been chosen to train the horses owned by Yugoslavian prime minister Marshal Tito. But he emigrated to Canada with his family in 1951. After moving to the United States, he worked for several trainers, and was assistant to Larry Geiger when he met Nerud, whose assistant, Mickey Walker, had recently died.

"I was very impressed with his knowledge of horses," Nerud said. "When I got back to the barn after talking with him, I said, 'Well, I just found my new assistant.' Joe could look at a horse and say, 'He's gonna be sick in a few days.' And he would be. I don't know how he knew, but he did. He was the best horseman I've ever been around and a wonderful guy."

Because of Nerud's no-speed policy in the mornings, Dr. Fager was not exactly the hottest news around the backstretch. Working every five days, he breezed an easy half in :49 from the gate on June 29, then came back on July 4 with five furlongs in a leisurely 1:03. On July 9, Nerud sent him a half from the gate, and the Doc showed a bit more speed, getting the distance in :48 2/5. As a final blowout for his first start, he went three furlongs in :37 on the Belmont training track.

Finally, it was time for his debut, a five and a half-furlong maiden race at Aqueduct on July 15. "I didn't know what the hell to expect from him," Nerud said. Never caring too much who rode his horses, he put apprentice rider David Hidalgo on. Hidalgo, who was under contract to Nerud, had been Dr. Fager's exercise rider back at

Tartan and also was his regular rider at the track. "Hell, anybody could ride him in his first start," Nerud said. "I just wanted to give the horse a race. I didn't care if he was first, second, or third."

He knew Hidalgo was as familiar with Dr. Fager as anyone. As he did with most first-time starters, he told the rider, "Now this horse probably isn't fit, so don't beat him up. Give him a chance." Hidalgo had no idea the Doc was anything special at that point, because he had never been asked to set him down before.

Nerud went up to his box, which he shared with a high-roller whom he knew simply as Ziggy. A field of eleven went to the gate, with Dr. Fager, breaking from post eight, at odds of nearly 11-1. With his slow works and a five-pound bug boy aboard, there was no indication the colt was anything out of the ordinary.

"So, is your horse gonna win?" Ziggy asked Nerud. "I ain't bettin' on him," Nerud replied. The trainer was nervous enough. He knew this could be the horse to silence his attackers in the McKnight organization. He'd been there for nine years, building up the operation. It was time for that one big horse to come along that would

launch Tartan Stable to the heights McKnight
and Nerud had envisioned.

"My whole future was riding on this horse,"
Nerud said. "I just wanted to see him run well and
show me the things he showed me in the mornings.
I knew he was a good horse, but you're scared to
death you've built your hopes up too high, and if
you're wrong you take an awful fall."

Ziggy's girlfriend told him she wanted to bet
twenty dollars on Dr. Fager. "Forget it; I'll book
it," Ziggy said. Nerud told him not to book any
bets on the horse. "Hell, you ain't bettin' him, so
I'm bookin' him," Ziggy said.

Dr. Fager lunged out of the gate, and Hidalgo
quickly grabbed a hold of him. Although he was
closer to the back of the pack than the front after
an opening quarter in :22 4/5, he was only three
lengths from the lead and starting to push horses
aside. Hidalgo, as he put it, was standing up
on him like a water skier just to keep him from
running over top of horses. Nearing the quarter
pole, Hidalgo ranged up alongside Walter Blum
on Richroband.

"I'm yelling 'Whoa,' on my horse, and I look
over and Blum is driving his horse," Hidalgo

recalled. "As I'm yelling 'Whoa,' I'm blowing by Blum. I couldn't believe it."

Dr. Fager drew off in the stretch and won under a hold. "It was all I could do to get him to only win by seven," Hidalgo said. His time of 1:05 was excellent over a very dead racetrack.

Ziggy, stunned by the performance, turned to Nerud and said, "You told me you weren't betting on him. Why didn't you bet this horse?" A relieved Nerud answered, "Look, Ziggy, I own a quarter of this horse, and if he's as good as I think he is, a hundred thousand one way or the other isn't gonna be that important."

When Hidalgo got back, he told his trainer, "Mr. Nerud, I've been working for you for three and a half years and I've never asked for a mount. Just let me ride this horse until I get beat." A nonchalant Nerud replied, "Sure, lad, you fit the horse well."

Up at Saratoga, Nerud had Hidalgo give Dr. Fager a good solid work to prepare him for a six-furlong allowance race. As they walked together from the Oklahoma training track to the main track, Nerud, sitting on his pony, told Hidalgo, "You're gonna be up against winners this time so have him running when you get to the pole and set him down for five-eighths of a mile."

"Well, I lit up to that pole," Hidalgo said. "And when I turned for home, I could see John jumping over the rail waving his arms at me. I'm standing straight up on the horse, but once you turn him loose there's no way you can shut him down. I thought I was gonna run right over John. As I went by, I could see him throw his hat, and I just yelled to him, 'Too late, boss.'"

The morning of the allowance race, Hidalgo went over to the jump riders, several of whom were in the hot box. There was always joking between the flat and jump riders, and Hidalgo said to them, "I'm riding a horse today, and if this sonofabitch gets beat, you guys can whup my ass one at a time."

Sent off at 4-5 in the eight-horse field, Dr. Fager broke well, and Hidalgo kept him in second to try to teach him to relax and get him used to dirt being kicked in his face. When he eased him out at the head of the stretch, the Doc easily opened a length lead. Hidalgo wondered what would happen if he hit him. "I reached back to hit him and he opened up by six before I had a chance to get my hand back on the rein," Hidalgo said.

But what the Doc also did was duck sideways from the whip. He resented being hit and always showed his displeasure at this foreign object. He cruised home with ease to win by eight lengths in 1:10 2/5, four-fifths of a second off the track record. But he was still upset over being whipped, and after the wire it took another half-mile before the outrider could get him pulled up.

Nerud was sitting in the box with one of his patrons, Harry S. Nichols, and when Dr. Fager pulled his little antic in the stretch, Nerud almost had a heart attack. He was so "shook up" afterward he had Nichols take his pulse some fifteen minutes after the race had been made official.

For Hidalgo, that was the last time he would ever ride Dr. Fager. When the overnights came out for the seven-furlong World's Playground Stakes at Atlantic City on September 10, Nerud informed Hidalgo he had named Manny Ycaza to ride. "Hidalgo realized this was a good horse and he decided he was gonna help me train him," Nerud said. "I thought he worked him too goddamn fast."

Hidalgo was crushed by the news. "He was the horse that was going to make my career," he said. "I'm still convinced if I had stayed on him he never would have gotten beat. I had been on him since he was a yearling and I had him down pat." Hidalgo told Nerud he still had a year left on his contract, but if he couldn't ride Dr. Fager, he didn't want to exercise him either, so he left to join Tartan's second-string in New Jersey. The following year, however, he would win the prestigious Man o' War Stakes aboard Tartan's Ruffled Feathers.

When Hidalgo saw Ycaza the day before the World's Playground, he told him, "Manny, be careful when you turn this horse on. When you let him loose, make sure you're clear, because you're not gonna be able to shut him off." Ycaza just glared at the brazen bug boy who was telling the veteran rider how to handle a horse.

"He started rattling off the names of all the big horses he'd ridden," Hidalgo said. "I just said to him, 'When you get back, you'll tell me he was the best horse you ever rode,' and I walked away."

Ycaza let Dr. Fager roll right out of the gate, and after battling through a half-mile in :45 2/5, the Doc found another gear and blew his field away, winning easily by twelve lengths. Three victories in three starts by a total of twenty-seven lengths.

"I met Manny at the clerk of scales when he got back," Hidalgo said. "He looked down at his shoes, then looked back up and said, 'You're right. That's a helluva horse.' "

But like Hidalgo, Ycaza's role as Dr. Fager's rider was short-lived, although he would be reunited the following year. Nerud, who had a long history with Bill Shoemaker, decided to take advantage of the Shoe's availability and named him to ride Dr. Fager in the seven-furlong Cowdin Stakes on October 5. A disgruntled Ycaza saw Hidalgo shortly after learning of the switch and said to him, "Don't tell Shoemaker anything." Hidalgo, still hoping he would one day be back on Dr. Fager, had no intentions of doing so.

Although Dr. Fager won the Cowdin, the race was a near-disaster. Shoemaker, noted more for his finesse than his strength, got left at the gate from the one-post. Nerud had told Shoemaker before the race, "Now, watch out for this goddamn horse." But when Shoemaker hit him, Dr. Fager took off and ran up into a wall of horses, banging his knee. Shoemaker had him under a pull, looking for running room, and when he finally did get clear, Dr. Fager came charging down the stretch and collared another Tartan Farm graduate, In Reality, in the final strides to win by three-quarters of a length. In Reality, who was owned by Frances Genter, would go on to become one of the best of his generation, and his battles with Dr. Fager were far from over.

After the Cowdin, Dr. Fager developed a filling in his knee where he had been struck in the Cowdin. Nerud was hesitant to run him in the one-mile Champagne Stakes, but decided to give it a shot. It was a decision he would come to regret. "I really didn't handle him very well that fall," Nerud said. "He had banged himself up pretty good in the Cowdin, and I never should have run him in the Champagne."

Shoemaker didn't ride Dr. Fager any better the second time around. The big colt was simply too strong for him, and was fighting with him through most of the race. Shoemaker tried to grab a hold of him, but a rank Dr. Fager eventually yanked him to the front and opened a three-length lead at the eighth pole. But his early efforts battling Shoemaker through a brutal half in :44 4/5 and three-quarters in 1:09 2/5 eventually took their toll. He began drifting out in the stretch, and Wheatley Stable's Successor, who had finished third behind Dr. Fager in the Cowdin, came charging out of the pack to win by a length, covering the mile in a sharp 1:35.

So, Dr. Fager's two-year-old campaign had come to an end. Successor would go on to win the rich Garden State Stakes to nail down the two-year-old championship. But a much more significant race took place three days before the Champagne. In the fifth race at Aqueduct, a seven-furlong maiden race was won in smashing style by Edith W. Bancroft's Damascus, sporting the famed Belair silks of her father William Woodward. Following his eight-length triumph, Damascus captured a seven-furlong allowance race by twelve lengths before squeezing through an opening on the rail to win the mile Remsen Stakes at Aqueduct by a length and a half. The stage was set for one of the most intense rivalries in racing history.

In recapping the year, Charles Hatton, noted writer for the *Daily Racing Form* and its sister publication *The Morning Telegraph*, said of Dr. Fager, "Whatever the future holds for Dr. Fager, he was exceptional as a two-year-old. It is seldom one sees a two-year-old of his height and scope who has the coordination to accelerate as he did."

Hatton added, "Betimes, Dr. Fager proved an astonishing performer, exciting the fans and leaving his rivals breathless."

But Hatton had seen only the tip of the iceberg. Over the next two years, it would be the entire racing world that Dr. Fager left breathless.

# Sword of Damascus

Racing in the early spring of 1967 was as vibrant and colorful as the newly blossomed crocuses and forsythias. The mighty Buckpasser, Horse of the Year of 1966, had already won the Malibu and San Fernando Stakes at Santa Anita, and was back in New York following an injury, gearing up for another run at the title. Meanwhile, one of the hottest crops of three-year-olds in years was gathering in Florida and New York to prepare for the long, arduous journey to Churchill Downs.

The big races in Florida were dominated by In Reality, winner of the Florida Derby, and an exciting newcomer on the scene named Reflected Glory, who had unleashed dramatic runs from the clouds to win the Everglades and Flamingo Stakes at Hialeah. The defending champ, Successor, was well behind the others and never would regain his two-year-old form.

Damascus came off a three and a half-month layoff to barely win a six-furlong allowance race at Pimlico, overcoming a severe bumping incident in the stretch. His trainer Frank Whiteley Jr. then brought him up to New York where he drew clear to win the seven-furlong Bay Shore Stakes by two and a half lengths in knee-deep mud for his fifth consecutive victory. Of all the three-year-olds seen up to that point, Damascus was far and away the brightest hope for the Kentucky Derby. He had the look of a classic horse, and he had the pedigree, being by Horse of the Year and Belmont Stakes winner Sword Dancer.

Unlike the tall, stately Dr. Fager and his hell-bent-for-leather approach to racing, and the bulldog-like In Reality, everything about Damascus screamed classics. In racing terminology, he was all hickory, and actually looked nothing like his sire. A brownish bay with black points, he would spring into action like a cat, and when he lowered his head and shoulders he seemed smaller than his sixteen hands. He had not yet shown the cannon-like move around the far turn that would become his trademark, but in future races he was a sight to behold, pouncing on his prey with one of the most devastating moves seen in many years.

So, as the one-mile Gotham Stakes approached, the only horse who looked capable of stopping the Damascus juggernaut was Dr. Fager. The Doc had been given a long vacation by Nerud, wintering at Hialeah, as he had done the previous year.

As spring approached, Dr. Fager still was far from a race. The colt had gotten bigger and stronger over the winter, but Nerud decided to take it easy with him, not wanting to gear him up too early. He never thought of Dr. Fager as a Kentucky Derby horse and spent a good deal of time getting that point across to McKnight, who naturally would have loved to have his first starter in the Run for the Roses. The Derby-hungry public and media couldn't understand Nerud's reluctance to give Dr. Fager at least a chance to show whether he was or wasn't Derby caliber.

Nerud finally found a solution. Whenever

someone inquired about Dr. Fager's status, he told him the colt had a variety of minor ailments, and he was forced to take it slowly with him. None of it was true. "I just gave them that crap because I didn't want to run the horse," Nerud said.

He did have Dr. Fager ready for a race before the Gotham, but couldn't find one. When he announced Dr. Fager would tackle Damascus in the Gotham off a six-month layoff, everyone thought he was out of his mind. But what other people thought never fazed Nerud in the slightest.

In addition to conceding a great deal of conditioning to Damascus, Nerud would have to find another jockey. Shoemaker was the regular rider of Damascus, and considered the colt one of the best he had ever ridden. It didn't bother Nerud one bit. He didn't like the way Shoemaker had ridden Dr. Fager in his two races, and preferred a rider who was a better fit for the horse.

"Shoemaker was the only jock who didn't fit him," Nerud said. "He and (Eddie) Arcaro were the two greatest riders I ever saw, but he was scared of Dr. Fager. He told me, 'John, this horse is too much for me.' He just didn't want to ride him."

Nerud went back to Manny Ycaza, who had won the World's Playground on Dr. Fager by twelve lengths the only time he rode him. "I was disappointed to be taken off him the previous year," Ycaza said, "but I knew Shoemaker was Nerud's guy. Before the Gotham, I heard that Shoemaker had told Nerud that Damascus was as good as any horse he had ever ridden. I don't think anyone should say that about a horse until he's proven himself."

So, Ycaza went Shoemaker one better. Always one to speak his mind and not be afraid to back it up, he told Nerud, "Well, in his mind, Damascus may be the best horse he's ever ridden, but I guarantee you I'll beat him."

To compensate for the lack of a prep race, Nerud scheduled a public workout for Dr. Fager between races at Aqueduct, in which he'd be accompanied by stablemates Aforethought (Dr. Fager's half-brother) and Gaylord's Feather. Dr. Fager sat back behind his workmates, then ran by them late to finish a length in front, while stopping the teletimer in a blistering 1:10 1/5.

Not many horses had been running that fast in races. The question was whether it would be enough to stop Damascus. One thing was obvious, people wanted to know the answer.

On a damp, foggy April afternoon, 50,522 fans jammed the Big A to see the first confrontation between Damascus and Dr. Fager. Although the Doc had been away for so long, they still couldn't separate the two horses, making them co-favorites at 13-10.

In the paddock, Nerud told Ycaza, "It doesn't matter where he is. Keep him wherever he wants to be. Just go along with him and he'll get him down on the money."

Damascus, one of the quickest horses out of the gate, broke like a bullet from the outside post in the field of nine. Ycaza put Dr. Fager in good position down on the inside. Longshot Royal Malabar was gunned to the lead by Angel Cordero Jr. and opened three lengths on the field as they headed into the far turn. Damascus was in second on the outside, with Ycaza keeping a close eye on him.

"I waited for Shoemaker the whole race, because of what he said about Damascus," Ycaza recalled. At the quarter pole, Royal Malabar was done and Shoemaker sent Damascus up to challenge. Ycaza had swung Dr. Fager out for clear sailing and moved up on Damascus' outside. The advantage Damascus had by breaking from the outside had disappeared, and he now found himself with this wild-eyed stranger bearing down on him.

The pair drew clear of the field, locked together as one. Unlike Dr. Fager, who always gave his all and never needed encouragement, Damascus had a tendency to loaf and needed to be woken up. Shoemaker would have liked to have gone to his right-hand whip, but the brute leaning in on him was too close, so he resorted to left-handed whipping. Dr. Fager stuck his head in front, then his neck. Damascus tried to battle back, but the Doc kept edging away. He hit the wire a half-length in front in the solid time of 1:35 1/5.

"It may sound like a strong statement, but I was toying with Damascus the whole race," said Ycaza. "I knew I had him whenever I wanted."

Shoemaker realized he had given Damascus a poor ride, staying too close to the pace and then giving up position. He went over to Whiteley after dismounting and said, "Frank, he beat him today, but he never will again as long as I ride him."

The Damascus-Dr. Fager rivalry had begun.

Nerud's assessment of the Gotham was much more simple: "It was a helluva good job of training." But now came the media pressure. Everyone was thinking Kentucky Derby for Dr. Fager...everyone but Nerud. Even Ycaza tried to convince him to point for the Derby. But Nerud, as he did with Gallant Man, stood his ground.

"After the Gotham, people knew he was capable of anything," Nerud said. Nerud's biggest antagonist after the race was *New York Daily News* racing columnist Gene Ward, who took up a crusade to get Dr. Fager to the Derby. "He started a campaign in the paper to get me to run him," Nerud recalled. "He kept saying we had to go to the Derby. I told McKnight that some newspaper men might be calling him asking why this horse isn't running in the Derby. I kept telling him he wasn't a Derby horse. It takes a certain type of horse to run in that race, and so many horses get killed trying to get there."

Instead of the Derby, Nerud pointed Dr. Fager to the one-mile Withers Stakes the week after. In the meantime, Damascus annihilated his opposition in the Wood Memorial, winning by six lengths and establishing himself as an overwhelming favorite for the Derby. But he was uncharacteristically rank early on the first Saturday in May and lacked his usual late punch, finishing third to longshot Proud Clarion. It has been said that Damascus became upset without his lead pony and close friend Duffy, who was not permitted to lead him to the post.

The Withers looked like it could be a good test for Dr. Fager, with the presence of the undefeated speedster Tumiga, who had just knocked off a field of top-class older horses in the seven-furlong Carter Handicap the week before. His trainer, Lucien Laurin, decided to wheel the son of Tudor Minstrel right back against Dr. Fager.

With Ycaza sitting out a suspension, Nerud was forced once again to look for a new rider for Dr. Fager. "I never gave a damn who rode him," he said. "He was such an amazing horse, I really believed no one had a chance against him."

He was able to get Braulio Baeza, who, along with Shoemaker on the West Coast, was the dominant rider in America. Baeza had first call for Eddie Neloy, who trained the powerful stables of Ogden Phipps, owner of Buckpasser, and Mrs. Henry Carnegie Phipps' Wheatley Stable, whose most notable star was Gallant Man's arch rival Bold Ruler. "John had tried to get me before to ride Dr. Fager, but I was always booked," Baeza said.

May 13th dawned bright and sunny, and once again a huge crowd of 50,233 showed up to see another possible slugfest. Dr. Fager's coat, still a bit dull in the Gotham, had improved dramatically in the four weeks since his debut. Dr. Fager, breaking from post eight on the far outside, was sent off as the 4-5 favorite, with Tumiga at 2-1. The Doc never seemed to have a problem rating early in races run out of a chute. He broke alertly and when Baeza took a hold of him, Dr. Fager came back to him willingly. But jockeys had to take advantage of Dr. Fager's congeniality while it lasted. And it usually didn't last long.

Tumiga, as he had done in the past, rocketed

to the lead through an opening quarter in :22 3/5, with Dr. Fager back in fourth, three lengths off the lead. Tumiga turned in a sensational second quarter in :21 3/5, getting to the half-mile pole in :44 1/5. Dr. Fager, as usual, tired quickly of being a spectator. He cut right into the teeth of that rapid quarter mile and collared Tumiga at the quarter pole. Both horses had blazed the six furlongs in an incredible 1:08, which was three-fifths of a second faster than Aqueduct's existing track record for the distance.

At this point, everyone normally would have been expecting another epic battle to the wire. But it was obvious that wasn't going to be the case. Tumiga was already in a full-out drive under Benny Feliciano, while Baeza, remarkably, was sitting motionless on Dr. Fager, the reins clutched up around his chest. Without the slightest bit of urging from Baeza, Dr. Fager roared by Tumiga and coasted home under wraps to win by six lengths in 1:33 4/5. Despite the ease of the victory, it still was the fastest mile ever run by a three-year-old in the history of New York racing.

The normally stoic Baeza jumped off Dr. Fager

and said to Nerud, "You better let me ride this horse. He's a machine."

Lucien Laurin, after watching his colt be destroyed by Dr. Fager, went over to Nerud and said, "I've got news for you. Your horse could have taken mine anytime he wanted to — and with those fractions!"

With another bravura performance by Dr. Fager, the cry of Preakness now resounded throughout the racing world. Nerud gave it a passing thought, but felt running back in one week was much too soon. He contemplated pointing for the Metropolitan Handicap, but when Buckpasser worked five furlongs in a sizzling :57 4/5 in his final prep for the race, Nerud decided it was too early to hook the champ. The Jersey Derby at Garden State Park was run the same day, and Nerud opted for the mile and an eighth race instead.

His only real threat in the Jersey Derby was In Reality, who had just finished second to Damascus in the Preakness. Damascus was back to his old self at Pimlico after his Derby failure, and his explosive move around the far turn blew the doors off In Reality and everyone else in the field, including Derby winner Proud Clarion. But In Reality did find another gear in the stretch and inched back a little at the wire to be beaten two and a quarter lengths.

With Baeza riding Buckpasser in the Metropolitan, Nerud went back to Ycaza. Although Nerud knew Dr. Fager was tons the best in the race, there was a nagging thought in the back of his mind. One of the stewards at Garden State was Keene Daingerfield, who Nerud said "didn't like me and hated Ycaza." In 1958, Daingerfield was one of the stewards who disqualified Ycaza from first in the Flamingo Stakes, putting up Calumet Farm's Tim Tam, and depriving Ycaza of his first $100,000 victory.

Ycaza had developed a dubious reputation for his aggressive riding, and Nerud knew, with Daingerfield present, he was sitting on a potential powder keg. That morning, when Ycaza awoke, he had a premonition that something bad was going to happen. No matter what he tried, he couldn't shake it. He still felt it as he drove to the track.

In the paddock before the race, Garden State owner Gene Mori walked over to Ycaza and told him, "Manny, now no incidents today. We've got the biggest crowd in the history of New Jersey racing. I don't want any trouble in this race."

Ycaza couldn't believe what he was hearing, and it just reinforced his feeling of dread. "It was unheard of for an owner of a track to do that," Ycaza said.

What made it all seem so ridiculous was that there were only four horses in the field and Dr. Fager was breaking from the outside. All Ycaza had to do was keep Dr. Fager out by himself going into the first turn and let him roll from there. Nerud told him to send the horse to the front. Ycaza was sure he could sit behind In Reality. He had heard that In Reality's trainer, Melvin (Sunshine) Calvert, had given jockey Earlie Fires instructions to go to the lead. "I don't want Sunshine's horse on the lead," Nerud shot back. "I want this horse on the lead."

Dr. Fager, favored at 3-10, broke quickly and Ycaza gunned him to the lead. What happened after that will always be a major subject of controversy. As Ycaza cut over entering the clubhouse turn, a traffic jam ensued inside him. First Air Rights and Gallant Moment bumped twice. Then In Reality, just inside Dr. Fager, was forced to steady and came in on both those horses at the seven-eighths pole. For a four-horse field, it was an ugly mess. Ycaza went about his business of getting Dr. Fager to the front, and once he accomplished that, the race was all but over. Dr. Fager steadily drew off after three-quarters in 1:10 3/5 and once again won eased up by six and a half lengths, covering the nine furlongs in 1:48, three-fifths off the track record.

The inquiry sign immediately went up, and in a few moments Dr. Fager's number came down, as runner-up In Reality was declared the winner. "He never touched any of those horses," Nerud said. "He was so much the best, and everyone was amazed they took him down."

"Ever since the Flamingo, that guy was always looking for something to give him an excuse to take my number down," Ycaza said. "I don't know the reason, but this was outrageous. I had him five off the rail, and he definitely was clear of those horses when I brought him in."

After the race, Nerud was quoted as saying the decision was prejudiced. He was then called in to the chief steward's office to explain himself.

When he was told there was rumor going around that he had said the Garden State stewards were prejudiced, Nerud said, "That ain't no rumor. That's what I said."

So, Dr. Fager had officially suffered his second career defeat. Nerud decided to go back to Baeza, marking the beginning of a long and successful partnership. "That was a double blow," Ycaza said. "First, getting disqualified, then getting taken off the horse. I felt bad enough about the disqualification, but I felt much worse getting taken off." He would get his revenge the following year.

The remainder of 1967 would go much smoother for Dr. Fager, with the exception of the Woodward Stakes, the epic match up which was to decide Horse of the Year. It was there another horse would come into Dr. Fager's life. Although not in the same league as the Doc, he would become a thorn in his side. His name was Hedevar.

# Bad Hare Day

In the summer of 1967, just prior to Dr. Fager's scheduled start in the Arlington Classic, there were major rumblings in the Tartan Stable organization. Tartan had been formed as a sub-chapter S corporation, which meant it could maintain the advantages of a corporation while being taxed as a partnership, where each partner is responsible for his own gains and losses. When Tartan was audited by the Internal Revenue Service, it was determined that the tax liability was greater than what was originally paid. As a result, Nerud found himself owing $250,000 in taxes, while McKnight owed his proportionate share. McKnight took the matter to court, and a settlement was made, where Nerud did not have to pay the penalty, but did have to give up his twenty-five percent interest in Tartan. He did, however, retain his interest in Dr. Fager.

"I didn't pay much attention to what it was all about," Nerud said. "I just left it up to the lawyers. And I really didn't give a damn about relinquishing my interest. I had plenty of horses and McKnight gave me certain considerations. So I wound up doing very well."

One of the reasons Nerud and McKnight became such a good team was that they were so much alike, especially about speaking their mind. Through Nerud's foresight and business acumen, McKnight wound up purchasing Tropical Park and part-interest in Hialeah. "He made $16 million on the Tropical deal," Nerud said.

Another reason for their success was McKnight's hands-off approach. He never called Nerud, who simply sent him a written progress report each week. McKnight was all business. After being together for twenty years, and with McKnight getting up there in years, Nerud told him, "McKnight, you're gettin' old. Why don't you will these horses to your daughter, so I know I'll have a job." A short while later, Nerud received a letter from McKnight, which read, "Dear Mr. Nerud, this is to inform you that I have transferred all my horses to my daughter's name. You are now taking orders from her."

"That was all it said," Nerud said. "Nothing like, it's been a lot of fun and I've enjoyed working with you over the years. Just a short form letter. But that was him. There was no bullshit about him. He once told me the secret to his success was just hard work and absolute faith in America. Give the people a product that can sell in every household in America, which he did."

Dr. Fager appeared nervous and edgy when he arrived in Chicago for the Arlington Classic following his first-ever plane trip. "He really didn't like flying," Nerud said, "but he learned to handle it well." Because he arrived so close to the race, Nerud decided not to give the colt a tranquilizer. Between the noise at the airport as he was being loaded and the six-hour trip, Dr. Fager was anxious to get off the plane.

A torrential downpour turned the track into a sea of slop the day of the race and Nerud was reluctant to run Dr. Fager. He told McKnight, "I'd rather be kicked in the balls than run this horse." When McKnight asked why he just didn't scratch him, Nerud said, "Look down that grandstand at all the people who came to see this horse run. I can't scratch him."

As it turned out, it wasn't even worth thinking about. Dr. Fager, sent off at 2-5, dueled for the early lead for a quarter of a mile, then turned the race into a procession. After opening up by two lengths through a lively half in :45, he left his opponents for dead, with Baeza sitting motionless on him, well off the rail. By the eighth pole, he was six in front, and at the wire, he had ten lengths on his closest pursuer, Lightning Orphan. Blue Grass Stakes winner Diplomat Way finished third in the six-horse field.

When Nerud was a young, up-and-coming trainer in New England, he decided he was going to leave Rockingham Park and try his luck on the New Jersey circuit. Rockingham president and chairman Lou Smith told Nerud before leaving, "Well, John, if you go broke, don't go to strangers." Nerud never forgot those words. As he departed, he thought, "That old sonof-abitch, I owe him something."

On July 15, 1967, it was payback time. As seven horses went to the post for the Rockingham Special, a $75,000 race which had been inaugurated the year before as a prep for the rich New Hampshire Sweepstakes Classic, among them was Dr. Fager. This move was frowned upon by many. On that same afternoon, Damascus was running in the prestigious ten-furlong Dwyer Handicap at Aqueduct. This would have been a perfect spot for the second meeting between these two giants of the Turf. Damascus had been on another roll following his Derby defeat, winning the Preakness, Belmont Stakes, and Leonard Richards Stakes. But a shocking nose defeat to the older Exceedingly in the William du Pont Jr. Handicap had Damascus and Frank Whiteley looking for redemption only a week later in the Dwyer. In the du Pont, Damascus was conceding eight actual pounds to Exceedingly and seventeen pounds on the scale.

Although another Dr. Fager-Damascus confrontation would have brought the fans out in droves, Nerud felt he had other priorities. "Old man Lou Smith was a wonderful guy, and I felt I owed him that," he said.

The nine-furlong Rockingham Special was nothing more than a workout for the 1-10 Dr. Fager, who cruised to a four and a quarter-length victory in 1:48 1/5, shattering the track record by a full second. Damascus, meanwhile, was involved in a much tougher battle. Carrying top weight of 128 pounds and conceding large chunks of weight over a deep, sloppy track, he turned in another of his rocket moves from last to first on the turn, making up a dozen lengths in the blink of an eye. But after turning for home, a stubborn Favorable Turn, in receipt of sixteen pounds, battled back. He fought Damascus throughout the stretch, as Shoemaker continued to lace into his colt. Damascus finally began to edge away, winning by three-quarters of a length.

The cry went up for a showdown in the Travers Stakes. Damascus went to Arlington for the mile and an eighth American Derby and broke the track record, annihilating In Reality by seven lengths in 1:46 4/5. One of the gladiators was primed and ready, but once again, it was not to be. Nerud decided instead to pass the Travers and head back up to Rockingham for the $250,000 New Hampshire Sweepstakes for Dr. Fager's first try at a mile and a quarter. Nerud, still unsure of Dr. Fager's distance capabilities, chose to bide his time and wait for the right moment before tackling a top-class stayer like Damascus.

His decision proved to be a wise one. Only three others showed up to face Damascus at Saratoga, and the track came up sloppy, making the ten furlongs even more demanding. Nerud must have breathed a sigh of relief when Damascus turned in one of the most devastating moves ever witnessed, coming from more than fifteen lengths back on the backstretch to win by a staggering twenty-two lengths, while equaling the track record.

Two weeks later, Dr. Fager traveled up to Rockingham for the Sweepstakes. But Nerud was worried. The colt hadn't been acting right and wasn't training with his usual enthusiasm. His temperature was normal, but Nerud knew he was far from a hundred percent. Dr. Fager, like many others in his family, was extremely susceptible to colic and had to be watched closely.

"There was nothing I could do," Nerud said. "I couldn't find anything physically wrong with him, and I knew, even not at his best, he'd still beat those horses."

Once again, his main threat appeared to be In Reality, who couldn't seem to find a race where he wasn't running into Damascus or Dr. Fager. Also in the field was Kentucky Derby runner-up Barbs Delight. Dr. Fager, favored at 1-5, went to the lead as expected, tracked by Barbs Delight and In Reality. After a half in :46 3/5, Earlie Fires, who had been in this unenviable position before on In Reality, decided he was going to try a bold and daring move to catch Dr. Fager by surprise. He steered his colt to the inside and attempted a sneak attack. As he charged up on Dr. Fager's inside, it was as if the Tartan colt became outraged at the unexpected intruder. Like any leader of the pack, he wasn't about to let this challenge go unanswered. As In Reality moved alongside Dr. Fager, the Doc reached over and attempted to take a chunk of hide out of In Reality's neck.

The two battled eyeball to eyeball for the next half-mile. Nerud knew the real Dr. Fager would have spit In Reality out by now, and that he was battling on guts alone. Inside the eighth pole, Dr. Fager finally got the better of In Reality and drew off to win by a length and a quarter. But it was obvious In Reality had run the race of his life when the teletimer stopped at 1:59 4/5, crushing Buffle's track record by an amazing three seconds. Nerud now knew Dr. Fager could handle ten furlongs with the best of them.

And that's exactly who he'd be facing in the Woodward Stakes. Was it finally about to happen? Called by many "The Race of the Century," the Woodward would be a battle royal between defending Horse of the Year Buckpasser and the three-year-old titans Damascus and Dr.

Fager. Also thrown in for good measure was the sometimes-brilliant Handsome Boy, who had destroyed Buckpasser by eight lengths in the Brooklyn Handicap.

But if there was any one factor that prevented the Woodward from being a true test of ability, it was the inclusion of two "rabbits," or pacesetters, who were entered by the connections of Damascus and Buckpasser for the sole purpose of cooking Dr. Fager. But from their viewpoint, Dr. Fager was the controlling speed in the race, and if left alone, he would be nearly impossible to catch. Handsome Boy had it in him to take the good doctor on, but his trainer Allen Jerkens was never one to be seen holding a loaded pistol to his head.

Buckpasser's rabbit, Great Power, didn't bother Nerud. Neloy had used pacesetters for Buckpasser a dozen times in the great horse's career, and Great Power didn't possess the speed and class of Impressive, who had set up Buckpasser's world-record mile at Arlington the previous year. But Damascus' pacesetter, Hedevar, was a different story. Hedevar, also owned by Edith Bancroft, jointly held the world record for a mile when Buckpasser broke it.

Nerud couldn't complain too much about the

rabbits, because he had used one himself for Gallant Man against Bold Ruler in the 1957 Belmont Stakes. "Rabbits will beat you," Nerud said. "But I didn't complain. I could have scratched him if I wanted. That other rabbit didn't mean anything, but Whiteley put a damn world-record holder in there."

With Baeza committed to ride Buckpasser, who had worked a brilliant mile and an eighth in 1:49 1/5 nine days before the race, Nerud decided to go with Bill Boland. "My big mistake was telling Boland to try to take back with him," Nerud said. "There was no way he was going to be able to take this horse back with those rabbits in there, so it was my mistake. It wasn't the first one I'd made."

Dr. Fager worked brilliantly for the race, breezing six furlongs in 1:12 3/5 on the deep Belmont training track eight days before, then blowing out a half in :47, also on the training track. Several days before the race, Nerud announced for the world to hear that if the Woodward had been a three-horse race it would be "no contest."

"This is supposed to be a race to decide the champion," he said. "Don't you think the champion should run on his own?"

When Shoemaker spoke to Whiteley the day

before the race, he told him, "You can run Hedevar if you want to, Frank, but I don't need him."

The publicity for the Woodward reached new highs in an era when only the local New York TV station, WPIX, televised non-Triple Crown races. There were no cap giveaways, no tote bags, no windbreakers. If there ever was a race that sold itself it was the 1967 Woodward. Never before had there been a race of this magnitude. Although no one knew it at the time, the Big Three would all be voted Horse of the Year, would all be inducted into the Hall of Fame, and would capture a combined thirteen championships. They equaled or broke eleven track records, including two world records, and won carrying 130 pounds or more twelve times. In eighty-five combined career starts, they won sixty-four races, fifty-four of them stakes.

A crowd of more than 55,000 showed up and made the Buckpasser entry the 8-5 favorite, with Dr. Fager and the Damascus entry both 9-5. Heavy rains the previous night had turned the track sloppy, but the sun and a cool autumn breeze helped turn it fast by post time. The opening eighth of a mile was a wild free-for-all. As luck, or the lack of, would have it, Dr. Fager drew post two, with the rabbits directly on either side of him. The Doc broke cleanly, and if Boland had any hopes of rating him, it died in the first hundred yards. As he grabbed the reins and attempted to shut down the revved-up engine beneath him, Bob Ussery, on Great Power, and Ron Turcotte, on Hedevar, began whipping and driving their horses, while screaming, as Boland put it, like a "bunch of wild Indians."

As Turcotte was giving Hedevar two right-handed smacks with the whip, Ussery stung Great Power four times in rapid succession. Turcotte then reached down and hit Hedevar two more times as they headed into the clubhouse turn.

"Mr. Neloy said to kill off Dr. Fager," Ussery said. "He just said go to the lead at all costs. I was trying to drop the horse to the front."

It was an incredible sight watching the speedsters Hedevar and Great Power in an all-out drive under the whip and still unable to outrun Dr. Fager, who was under a stranglehold by Boland. After an opening quarter in :22 2/5, Great Power quickly threw in the towel, but Hedevar stuck with Dr. Fager. Boland had already lost control of the Doc and was now merely a passenger. The pair whizzed past the three-quarter pole in :45 1/5, as Damascus and

Buckpasser bided their time, more than a dozen lengths off the suicidal pace. Even the normally quick-footed Handsome Boy was unable to keep up.

Dr. Fager, now hurtling down the backstretch with his mouth open, finally put Hedevar away and opened a clear lead, but the damage had been done. He had blazed the opening three-quarters in a brutal 1:09 1/5, and Damascus and Buckpasser were already closing in for the kill. At the quarter pole, Dr. Fager was cooked. Damascus, crouched low, pounced on him, and quickly burst clear. Buckpasser was making a belated rally, but his only hope was for second. Damascus continued to pour it on. A rare come-from-behind horse who had the power and the desire to decimate his foes, he drew off to a spectacular ten-length victory, with Buckpasser just getting the better of a weary Dr. Fager for second. The time was a solid 2:00 3/5. There was no question who the Horse of the Year was.

A totally frustrated Nerud approached New York Racing Association chairman James Cox Brady after the race and said, "You tell them I'll put up $50,000 and the Association will put up $50,000. Winner-take-all, Dr. Fager against Damascus. They (Damascus' connections) put up nothing."

But Brady quickly nixed the idea.

Nerud then set his sights on the mile and a quarter Hawthorne Gold Cup three weeks later, while Damascus awaited the two-mile Jockey Club Gold Cup the following week. *The New York Times* sports editor Jim Roach flew out to Chicago with Nerud. Although Nerud brought his own nightwatchman, he wanted additional security on the scene. "I was in Chicago," he said.

Nerud went straight to Hawthorne managing director Robert Carey, informing him he wanted to be supplied a security guard. When the stable manager's son was recruited, Nerud told him, "Don't come empty. Make sure you come with a damn six-shooter." A short while later, a limo pulled up to the barn and several men in suits got out and asked to see Dr. Fager. The regular nightwatchman told them they couldn't go in the barn without Nerud's permission.

"They obviously wanted to stop the horse," Nerud said, "and they thought they looked like big shots with their suits and limo. But when they started to walk in the barn anyway, the manager's son pulled out his six-shooter, with a barrel a mile long, and stuck it right in the guy's belly. 'You heard what the man said,' he told them. They turned and went back in the limo and got the hell out of there. When Roach came by the barn and wanted to know what had happened, this kid took out the gun and stuck it in Roach's belly to show him. Hell, my watchman couldn't have stopped them by himself. When I asked Roach if he was gonna write about it, he said no way."

With that incident behind him, Nerud sent Dr. Fager to the post for the Gold Cup. About an hour and a half before the race, Nerud learned he had won the Man o' War Stakes with Ruffled Feathers. In the Gold Cup, the 3-10 Dr. Fager got caught up in another speed duel, this time with the quick Whisper Jet. The pair churned out solid fractions of :46 1/5 and 1:10 1/5. After a mile in 1:35 1/5, Whisper Jet, in receipt of nine pounds, was still at Dr. Fager's throat, but the good doctor was under an easy hold by Baeza. When they turned for home, Dr. Fager opened up on his own and drew off to a two and a half-length victory.

A week later, Damascus romped in the Jockey Club Gold Cup, and although he was later beaten a nose by Fort Marcy in the Washington, D.C. International in his first grass attempt, it didn't diminish the remarkable year he had had. He had made sixteen starts, winning twelve, with three seconds and a third.

Nerud had contemplated putting Dr. Fager away for the year, but decided to drop him back in a sprint in the seven-furlong Vosburgh Handicap. Baeza kept Dr. Fager wide throughout, then pointed him for home and let the horse do the rest. He cruised by the hard-knocking Jim J. leaving the eighth pole and went on to a four and a half-length score in a snappy 1:21 3/5, just two-fifths off the track record.

So, Dr. Fager's three-year-old campaign ended with seven victories in nine starts, with one of his two defeats coming at the hands of the stewards. He was voted champion sprinter in the *Morning Telegraph/Daily Racing Form* poll, which was the recognized poll since championships were started. In two years of racing, his average winning margin was five lengths.

What would his four-year-old campaign bring? To what intensity would his rivalry with Damascus grow? Those were the questions fans were asking at the end of 1967. While Damascus would go on to further glory in the handicap ranks, no one in their wildest imagination could have envisioned what awaited them in 1968.

# The Freak Show Begins

Webster defines the word freak as "Any abnormal person, animal or plant," with abnormal meaning, "Not normal; not average; not typical." Considering that in 1968, Dr. Fager was anything but normal, average, or typical, it is safe to say he was a freak.

There is no way to explain what transformations take place in a Thoroughbred from one year to the next. But the Dr. Fager who emerged from his winter quarters at Hialeah in the spring of 1968 was a different creature from the one racing fans had seen the previous two years. From the classy and incredibly fast colt who had seemingly found his niche on the racetrack came a horse who looked like no one, who ran like no one, and who displayed a combination of speed, tenacity, versatility, and weight-carrying ability never before seen.

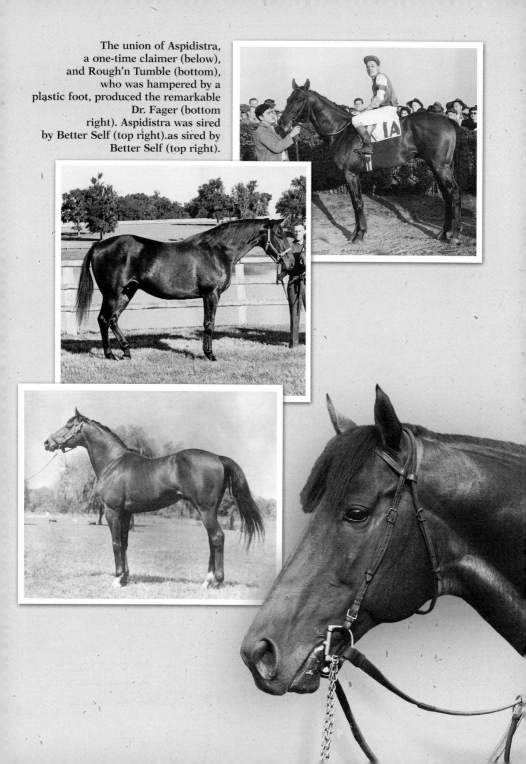

The union of Aspidistra, a one-time claimer (below), and Rough'n Tumble (bottom), who was hampered by a plastic foot, produced the remarkable Dr. Fager (bottom right). Aspidistra was sired by Better Self (top right).as sired by Better Self (top right).

An aerial view of Tartan Farm, which encompassed more than 1,000 acres, and one of the yearling barns and farm signs (top). The group of Tartan yearlings (right) shows Dr. Fager on the lead, with In Reality alongside. Other yearlings in the set include Ruffled Feathers and Minnesota Mac.

Dr. Fager winning the Cowdin Stakes (top); Dr. Fager's first jockey, David Hidalgo, owner William McKnight, and trainer John Nerud (above); Nerud checking equipment (left) before sending out the Doc.

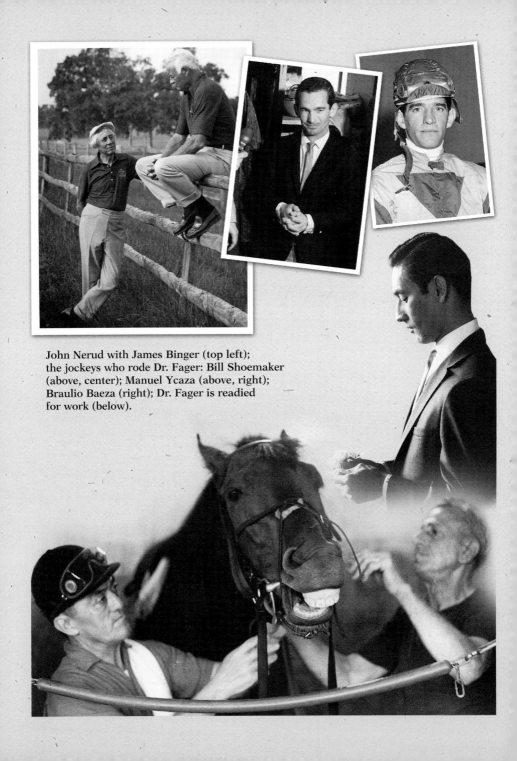

John Nerud with James Binger (top left);
the jockeys who rode Dr. Fager: Bill Shoemaker
(above, center); Manuel Ycaza (above, right);
Braulio Baeza (right); Dr. Fager is readied
for work (below).

Dr. Fager defeats his rival, Damascus, in the Gotham (above); the Doc dominates in a public six-furlong workout (left) in a prep for the Gotham; working out before the Gotham with regular exercise rider Jose Marrero in the irons.

Dr. Fager is led to the winner's circle after his victory in the Withers (above); although he won the Jersey Derby (below), Dr. Fager was disqualified and placed last for interference on the first turn. In Reality was declared the winner.

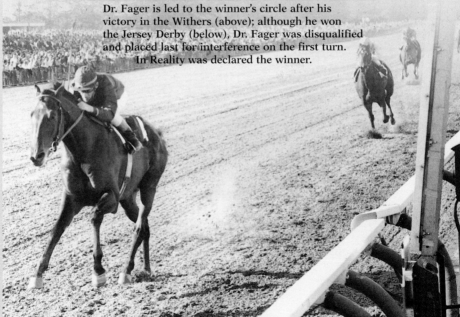

Dr. Fager easily winning the
Arlington Classic (top);
working as the new Belmont
Park takes shape (above);
morning routine (left).

Getting toweled off by exercise rider Jose Marrero (right); standing (center) with assistant trainer Spasoje Dimitrijevic on his left, hotwalker John Peterka on his right, and one of Tartan's grooms Dusan Gojkovic on his far right; working (below) with Jose Marrero up.

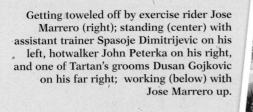

Dimitrijevic leading Dr. Fager into the winner's circle after the Suburban Handicap (top); in the post parade (left) with Baeza up and Jose Marrero on Chalkeye, the pony; on the lead in |the Suburban (below) with Damascus behind and to the right; beaten by his nemesis, Damascus, in the Brooklyn (bottom).

Dr. Fager setting his world-record mile, 1:32 1/5, in the
Washington Park Handicap at Arlington Park;
with John Nerud and exercise rider Jose Marrero (left);
winning the Whitney at Saratoga (top).

Dr. Fager posing for sculptress Katherine Thayer Hobson (above); winning the Vosburgh (right) by six lengths; closing on the outside for a narrow victory in the United Nations Handicap (below).

Led by John Nerud, Dr. Fager leaves Belmont Park for stud duty at Tartan Farms; (above) he is issued a "citation" for speeding.

Enjoying the expanse of his paddock (above); returning to her birthplace, champion Ta Wee (right) is greeted by her dam, Aspidistra (on the left), and her half-brother Dr. Fager; going for a quiet hack in 1974 (below).

Son Dr. Patches winning the 1978 Vosburgh (top); descendant Unbridled coming home first in the 1990 Kentucky Derby (above); and champion daughter Dearly Precious (left) after winning the 1975 Sorority Stakes.

Despite his untimely end,
Dr. Fager remains Tartan Farms'
most accomplished son.

DR. FAGER
B.H. 1964 — 76
"ROUGH'N TUMBLE - ASPIDISTRA

RACING'S GRAND
'68 HORSE OF THE Y
HANDICAP CHAMPI
SPRINT CHAMPION
GRASS CHAMPION
WORLD RECORD OF 1 MILE 1:32

His feats that year would transcend Thoroughbred racing. He not only raised the equine genus to another level, it would be difficult to find a human athlete who set such lofty standards over the course of a single year. Every track and field record that existed in 1968 was erased long before Dr. Fager's records fell. Although racing would be graced by three Triple Crown winners and countless superstars, it would take three decades finally to crack through the seemingly impenetrable wall Dr. Fager built. Many came within a whisper of it, but like the Doc himself, it was like trying to catch the wind.

It was a quiet winter for Dr. Fager. He was given a three-week vacation just walking the shed before being put back in light training. In the beginning, he'd walk a day, then gallop a day until Nerud felt it was time to pick up the tempo. A problem with his right knee, then an ankle, put him behind schedule. On Nerud's horizon was another showdown with Damascus. All he wanted was an opportunity to match the two colts against each other without a rabbit. But Frank Whiteley knew what the consequences would be and wasn't about to hand Dr. Fager any races on a silver platter.

Unlike Dr. Fager, Damascus thrived on racing and didn't need much time to get over his grueling sixteen-race three-year-old campaign. Less than two months after his nose defeat in the Washington, D.C. International, he was in California and ready for action. Following victories in the Malibu and San Fernando Stakes and a head defeat over a deep, heavy track in the Charles H. Strub Stakes, Damascus was sent back East to Whiteley's base at Delaware Park. Dr. Fager, meanwhile, still was three months from a race.

In Reality, with six victories and six seconds in twelve starts in 1967, had been put away in September by Sunshine Calvert and was brought back for a Florida campaign. He showed moderate success, coming away with only a pair of thirds in the Royal Palm and Seminole Handicaps. But In Reality's best days were ahead of him.

With Damascus still resting down at Delaware for what would be a rare five-month vacation, Dr. Fager started gearing up for his long-awaited four-year-old debut. With Buckpasser retired, Baeza was all his. Well, almost all his. Nerud targeted the seven-furlong Roseben Handicap at Aqueduct for Dr. Fager's first race.

Unfortunately, that was run the same day as the Kentucky Derby, in which Baeza was riding Iron Ruler. Nerud dipped into the jockey pool and came up with "Gentleman" John Rotz, one of the most dependable riders on the circuit.

As the race neared, Nerud wanted to provide the fans with a sneak preview of the new and improved Dr. Fager, while giving Rotz a chance to get acquainted with the horse. He scheduled a five-furlong workout between races with Rotz aboard. The rider was in for a rude awakening. This was Dr. Fager's time of day, and he knew afternoons with people in the stands meant putting on a show. With the Doc's long mane blowing in his face, Rotz just sat on him and never moved his hands. He couldn't believe it when he was told the colt had worked in :56 4/5. The only word that came to mind as he dismounted was "phenomenal."

With Dr. Fager now bigger and stronger and wilder, Nerud decided to have him look the part, so he let his mane and forelock grow over the winter. "It was a great show," he said. "The way it waved in the wind, it made him look a like a wild horse."

The wild horse made a mockery of the Roseben, although Nerud didn't want anything so spectacular that it would start turning the heads of Tommy Trotter and other racing secretaries. He was already starting the year off with 130 pounds, with an entire campaign of handicap races ahead of him. He was sent off at 1-5 against his old friend from the Withers, Tumiga, who was back for another crack at the Doc after winning the Cherry Hill Handicap at Garden State Park in a dazzling 1:08 4/5 to equal the track record.

Tumiga attempted to run with Dr. Fager, but like in the Withers, he couldn't get him to break a sweat. After a half in :45, Dr. Fager drew off, with Rotz pulling back on the throttle, way up in the saddle. He knew he couldn't let the Doc win by too much with the heavy-handed Mr. Trotter watching. It was all he could do to get him to win by only three lengths. Dr. Fager crossed the wire with his ears straight up, stopping the teletimer in 1:21 2/5, just one-fifth off the track record set six years earlier by Rose Net under 114 pounds.

After the race, Nerud sent a message to Trotter through the press. "I'd like to run him in the Metropolitan Handicap, if they let me," he said jokingly. But first he needed to get another race in Dr. Fager. The seven-furlong Carter Handicap was a possibility. But shortly after the Roseben, Nerud received a call from Hollywood Park racing secretary Jack Meyers, informing him that under the allowance conditions of the May 18 Californian Stakes, Dr. Fager would only have to carry 124 pounds.

Nerud decided to go, and put Dr. Fager on a plane for his first cross-country trip. When he arrived, however, he discovered there had been a miscalculation, and that Dr. Fager actually had to carry 130 pounds. But Nerud had come to run. "If he's got thirty, he's got thirty," he said.

The Californians had their own speedball, named Kissin' George, who was coming off three straight brilliant sprint victories. At the current meet, he had won the six-furlong Premiere Handicap in 1:08 3/5 and a division of the seven-furlong Los Angeles Handicap in 1:21 1/5. But Kissin' George was strictly a sprinter, and although he posed little threat to Dr. Fager at the mile and a sixteenth distance of the Californian, he certainly could do damage if Dr. Fager hooked up with him early.

Also in the field was the fast and classy Rising Market, who had finished second to

Kissin' George in the Premiere before winning the other division of the Los Angeles Handicap in 1:20 3/5. Earlier in the year, he had finished second to Damascus in the Malibu and won the nine-furlong San Antonio Stakes. Another horse to contend with was the great filly Gamely, who was destined for the Hall of Fame.

With the presence of Kissin' George, twelve others showed up to take advantage of the imminent suicidal speed duel. Their confidence swelled when Dr. Fager drew post eleven.

In the saddling stall, Dr. Fager was restless, tossing his head around and working up a mouthful of saliva. The longer he waited, the more agitated he became. He began pawing at the ground, first with the right foot, then the left. His groom, Joe Findley, held him on one side, while Nerud kept pushing against him from the other side, all the while talking to him.

When the gates opened, Dr. Fager broke cleanly, but took about fifty yards to get in gear. Kissin' George, meanwhile, broke like a bullet and sprinted to the front. Dr. Fager was running freely, about four off the rail, going into the clubhouse turn. As they turned into the backstretch, Dr. Fager, under restraint from Baeza, was still in fourth, but running like the wild horse Nerud had intended him to look like. With his head up and mouth open, he was literally leaping in the air, flip-flopping his leads. A weary-armed Baeza realized he was fighting a lost cause. When a gaping hole opened along the rail, Dr. Fager dragged Baeza in there. He then set his sights on Kissin' George and took off after him.

After dueling around the far turn, the six furlongs in 1:08 3/5, Dr. Fager drove Kissin' George into the ground and quickly opened a four-length lead in mid-stretch. Baeza then gave Dr. Fager one little right-handed love tap with the whip, and the Doc's tail shot straight up like a geyser. He jumped back onto his left lead, causing him to duck in. Baeza then wisely hand-rode him the rest of the way, crossing the wire three lengths in front of Gamely, while covering the mile and a sixteenth in 1:40 4/5. No horse had ever carried that much weight to win the Californian.

After the Californian, Nerud decided to equip Dr. Fager with a figure-eight bridle to give Baeza better control over him. He put the colt back on a plane and headed home to prepare for the

Met Mile, which was only twelve days away. Facing him would be In Reality, who also had gone through a major transformation. After arriving up north from Florida, In Reality had easily won a prep for the prestigious John B. Campbell Handicap at Bowie, setting a new track record, before winning the Campbell over Barbs Delight. He then knocked off Tumiga in the Carter Handicap, zipping the seven furlongs in 1:21 4/5.

Whether it was the trip to California or not, on the eve of the Metropolitan, Dr. Fager came down with a severe case of colic. This had always been a concern to Nerud, considering Aspidistra was always susceptible to it, and eventually would lose many of her foals to colic.

Dr. Fager had returned from a gallop that morning and appeared in distress. Nerud summoned veterinarian William O. Reed, who gave the colt a normal dose of relaxant and tranquilizer. But it didn't help. Dr. Fager was in terrible agony. "He was literally banging his head against the wall," Nerud recalled. "I thought we had lost him." Dr. Fager tried to go down, but several men held him up, knowing if he did go down, there was a good chance he'd never get up. Dr. Reed wound up giving him three times the normal dose of relaxant. He was such a strong, rugged horse, normal doses had little effect on him. Finally, he began to settle down and in a short while he was calm. He came out of it fine, but the ordeal would force him to miss the Met Mile and knocked him out for a couple of weeks.

With Dr. Fager on the sidelines, In Reality had little trouble winning the Met over Advocator in 1:35. It had been a special spring in New York that year with the re-opening of the new Belmont Park, which had closed after the 1962 season to allow construction of a new grandstand. What kind of standards a healthy Dr. Fager would have set going a flat mile over a spanking new surface one can only imagine.

The next act in the unfolding drama came on June 17 when Frank Whiteley put Damascus in a mile and seventy-yard allowance race at Delaware Park to get a nice easy race in him for the long, hard grind that was sure to follow. Sent off at 1-10, Damascus just toyed with his overmatched foes to win by almost four lengths easing up, while missing the track record by two-fifths of a second.

The battle lines were now drawn. Dr. Fager, Damascus, and In Reality were on a collision course that would bring them face to face on the Fourth of July in the mile and a quarter Suburban Handicap. But of the three, only In Reality had been racing hard over the past two months. Could Dr. Fager be fully wound after a nearly seven-week layoff and coming so close to dying? Was the rugged Damascus ready to lock horns with Dr. Fager coming off only one easy allowance victory in five months? Also, pointing for the race was the vastly improved George D. Widener-owned colt Bold Hour, who had won his last two starts, including the Grey Lag Handicap at Aqueduct.

On the Monday before the race, Tommy Trotter received a call from Frank Whiteley informing him that Damascus definitely would be coming, but he would not be coming alone. Accompanying him would be Hedevar. To Nerud, it looked as if Dr. Fager would never get a chance to go one-on-one with his arch rival, and he made it a point to let everyone know that the decision just reaffirmed his belief that Damascus' connections thought they could not beat Dr. Fager without help.

Trotter now had the chore of weighting both horses. He gave Damascus top weight of 133 pounds, with Dr. Fager 132 and In Reality 125. Trotter said it was the first time he could recall weighting two horses that high for the same race. Hedevar was assigned 112.

On the morning of the race, Nerud and Sunshine Calvert were in the racing office joking around about the presence of Hedevar. But they spoke only half in jest. In Reality was a stalker, and there was a question whether a rabbit would help or hurt him. Later that morning, Nerud was still there when Whiteley walked in to see Trotter. As he emerged from behind the counter, Nerud, sitting there minding his own business, overheard a jockey's agent say that Whiteley had just scratched Hedevar. When Whiteley looked over at Nerud and didn't deny it, Nerud knew it was true. He stood up and said to no one in particular, "Well, the race is over."

As the huge crowd of more than 54,000 was settling into their seats, the familiar high pitched voice of track announcer Fred Capossela resounded over the loudspeaker. "Ladies and gentlemen," he announced, "in the seventh race, number 1A

Hedevar has... been... scratched." The murmur that went up seemed to carry all the way to Jamaica Bay. Hedevar, it was reported, had taken a few bad steps following a six-furlong workout, and Whiteley didn't want to take any chances running him.

Charles Hatton described the situation best when he later wrote in the *Daily Racing Form* and *Morning Telegraph*, "Then, Hedevar took a couple of bad steps, and trainer Frank Whiteley Jr. took the hasenpfeffer out of Nerud's cabbage."

Yes, the rabbit was gone from the stew. It was Dr. Fager and Damascus once and for all. Dr. Fager looked better than ever in the paddock. He had really filled out into his long frame and long legs, and he walked around with his head high as if he ruled the world. Damascus' coat was beaming, and although he might have been carrying a bit more flesh than normal, he was on his toes and ready for action.

The fans made Dr. Fager the 4-5 favorite, with Damascus 7-5. Completing the five-horse field was the hard-hitting filly Amerigo Lady. Riding Damascus was none other than Dr. Fager's old pilot Manny Ycaza, who was replacing the injured Bill Shoemaker.

At the start, Damascus, as usual, broke quickest of all. But in a few strides, Dr. Fager was all over him. With his long mane blowing wildly in the warm summer breeze, the Doc cruised by Damascus, as Baeza just buried his head in the colt's mane and let him loose. He gave a peek to his left to make sure he was clear of Damascus before easing over to the rail. With no one to get his blood boiling, Dr. Fager rated beautifully on his own, opening up a two-length lead around the clubhouse turn.

In Realty had broken on his wrong lead and apparently taken a bad step, causing a minor injury that would lead to his retirement. He tried to stay in the race, but was never a factor. That left Damascus on a solo mission. Ycaza could either sit back and let Dr. Fager control the race or take the initiative and try to crack him early. He chose the latter. It actually was a no-brainer, as Dr. Fager already had crawled his opening quarter in :24 and still was on cruise control through a half in :48 2/5.

Ycaza took Damascus off the rail and started pushing hard. This wasn't Damascus' kind of race, but in typical cat-like fashion, he pounced on Dr. Fager down the backstretch. The battle everyone had wanted to see for so long was on. Damascus pulled to within Dr. Fager's throatlatch, then hit a brick wall. The Doc seemed to relish the challenge and refused to let Damascus get any closer. With his initial attack thwarted, Ycaza regrouped and let Damascus catch his breath. Then he lowered his head and shoulders and started pushing hard. This time, Damascus charged up and looked the tiger right in the eye. The pair had just run their third quarter in a brutal :22 3/5.

Dr. Fager, with his head still up, seemed to dwarf Damascus, who was stretched out like a string. This time, the Doc wasn't playing around. He knew he was in for a fight. As hard as Ycaza pushed, he and Damascus couldn't get by the tenacious Dr. Fager. Around the turn, Dr. Fager began inching away, putting a half-length between him and his attacker. But, amazingly, Damascus wasn't through yet. He came charging back for the third time and might actually have gotten his nose in front. They had flown around the turn in :23 3/5 and came to the quarter pole locked together. The roar from the crowd was deafening.

Dr. Fager refused to yield. His flared nostrils might as well have had smoke blowing from them.

His glaring eyes could easily have had daggers shooting from them. As they turned for home, a weary-legged Damascus finally began to crack. Dr. Fager bounded clear, opening up by two lengths, getting the mile in 1:34 3/5. Bold Hour, who had been eyeing the battle, came on to try to pick up the pieces. In receipt of sixteen and seventeen pounds, he collared Damascus and set his sights on Dr. Fager. But Baeza was sitting still on the Doc and merely hand rode him to the wire to win by two lengths. Despite the sluggish opening half, Dr. Fager had equaled Gun Bow's track record of 1:59 3/5.

After the race, a jubilant and vindicated Nerud said, "There's never been a race in my life that did me as much good."

Whiteley felt Damascus needed the race and decided to run him back nine days later in the Amory L. Haskell Handicap at Monmouth. Carrying 131 pounds and conceding fifteen pounds to Bold Hour, Damascus stumbled badly at the start and never showed his big kick, finishing third behind Bold Hour and Mr. Right. But the colt seemed to blossom with each race, and Whiteley was confident he had him in peak condition for the Brooklyn Handicap the following week. By now, Hedevar had recovered from his ailment and was ready for his search and destroy mission. The hasenpfeffer was back on the menu.

But Trotter thought the new Dr. Fager was over his disdain of rabbits. "I think he's an entirely different horse this year," he said before the race. "He can be rated and save something for the end, even if speed goes with him. I don't think the rabbit can bother him now."

For the Brooklyn, Trotter lowered Damascus to 130 pounds, but raised Dr. Fager three pounds to 135. Nerud didn't bat an eye. He always remembered the words of the great Hirsch Jacobs: "If you think the secretary put too much weight on your horse, just run him. If he gets beat, he'll take some off. And if he wins, then he had him weighted right."

"It was that simple," Nerud said. "I never argued about weight. That's the way handicapping is, and that's part of racing. I've always said there should be no handicaps in grade two and grade three races. But what are you going to do? I wasn't worried about the weight. He would have won even with that weight if it weren't for the rabbit."

Nerud thought about having Baeza just try to outrun Hedevar, but decided it wasn't in the colt's best interests, so he had him take a hold of him. Dr. Fager had matured since the Woodward, and judging by the Suburban, he certainly had the ability to slow the pace down. But that was when he was running freely by himself. What would happen with Hedevar blasting out of there? A rank Dr. Fager with 135 pounds up was the last thing Nerud wanted.

One look at Damascus in the paddock and it was obvious he had progressed since the Suburban. He pranced around on his toes with his neck arched and his muscles ready to explode. Hedevar, breaking from the outside post in the seven-horse field, burst out of the gate under jockey Tommy Lee, who immediately looked over to his inside to see where Dr. Fager was. The Doc was under a double stranglehold by Baeza and already climbing, trying to fight him. Before Lee knew it, he was three lengths in front. He had launched a missile and had no target to hone in on. Baeza continued to pull hard on Dr. Fager in an effort to keep him away from Hedevar. Ycaza, meanwhile, had Damascus well back in the pack, where he liked to be.

Lee's instructions were to carve out a fast pace for Damascus, and that's what he did. He zipped the opening half in :45 4/5, with Dr. Fager a length and a half back. That's 2 3/5 seconds faster than Dr. Fager had run in the Suburban. And this time he was lugging 135 pounds. Inside the five-eighths pole, Baeza, back in the saddle and legs straight as an arrow, no longer had any say in the matter and was forced to let Dr. Fager go. He blew by Hedevar and quickly opened a five-length lead. But the Doc was out of control, his three-quarters in a blistering 1:09 2/5, while Damascus was now in full gear and flying.

At the quarter pole, Damascus' electrifying move already had him lapped on Dr. Fager in 1:34 3/5 for the mile. Between the weight and fighting Baeza through those suicidal fractions, the Doc was spent. He tried to come back at Damascus, but he was up against a fresh horse who was just beginning to run. Baeza cracked Dr. Fager twice right-handed, and once again he threw his tail up in defiance. He was tired and still trying and didn't need any further encouragement at that point. Damascus drew clear to win by two and a half lengths, and his time of 1:59 1/5 took two ticks off the record that Dr. Fager had equaled sixteen days earlier. The amazing aspect of the victory was that it was Damascus' third race in sixteen days, all carrying 130 pounds or more.

Nerud, as expected, spouted off about the use of Hedevar, but admitted, "I've got my opinions, that's the truth. But sometimes, I'd be better off if I kept my mouth shut."

Whiteley's comment, as usual, was plain and to the point. "Hedevar did a helluva job, as far as he went."

Dr. Fager lost nothing in defeat. Sadly, it would be the last time these two great horses would ever meet. Damascus would add two more victories before tailing off due to a variety of unspecified ailments. His remarkable career would end ignominiously in the Jockey Club Gold Cup, where he struggled to the wire, beaten nearly forty lengths. He had suffered a bowed tendon and was retired to stud at Claiborne Farm, where he became a prolific sire of stakes horses, living to the age of thirty-one.

Dr. Fager's four-year-old campaign was now half over, and although he had already established himself as one of the greats of his era, he was about to catapult to heights never before attained.

# By Which All Others Are Measured

It was one of those overcast, humid Saratoga mornings when you knew it was just a matter of time before the skies opened up. On the track, horses were winding down their morning's activities, while patrons in the clubhouse dining area behind the apron were finishing off their breakfasts. It was a grand time to be in Saratoga. Mornings were a feast for the senses — a golden sunrise illuminating the half-mile pole; the nation's top horses barreling down the stretch in succession; the clanging of dishes; and the smell of bacon and coffee permeating throughout the clubhouse.

With the Travers Stakes to be run that afternoon, a larger crowd than usual had showed up to partake in this daily Saratoga ritual, where fans and horsemen mingled over breakfast, and where the tips usually were hotter than the eggs. As the morning wore on, and with most of the horses back in their barns, an imposing figure emerged from the tunnel, accompanied by an Appaloosa pony named Chalkeye. With Jose Marrero aboard, the mighty Dr. Fager stepped on the track for his five-furlong breeze that would be his final major work for the following week's Washington Park Handicap.

Two weeks earlier, the Doc had turned the prestigious Whitney Stakes into nothing more than a stroll in the park. Only three others showed up for the mile and an eighth race, and none of them could even begin to warm up Dr. Fager, despite the lopsided weight differential. Under the allowance conditions, Dr. Fager had to carry 132 pounds compared to 114 for the others. But the fans still sent him off at odds of 1-20. The only function Baeza served on that day was to make sure Dr. Fager had a rider on his back when he crossed the finish line. It was that easy. Baeza kept the Doc out in the middle of the track the whole way, cruised through fractions of :47 1/5 and 1:11 3/5, then sat on him through the stretch as if he were in a lounge chair back home watching TV. Dr. Fager drew off on his own to win by eight lengths in 1:48 4/5.

As soon as Dr. Fager stepped foot on the track,

a loud clap of thunder rocked Saratoga. It was as if the gods were announcing his arrival. Marrero, dressed in a red pullover shirt, enhanced the image of the Doc donned in his familiar Tartan silks. Weighing more than 150 pounds, Marrero provided enough weight to keep the Doc's works under control. As he made his way along the rail, the rains came, as only Saratoga rains could. Under the grandstand, Nerud, anticipating the downpour, was decked out in a yellow poncho. As the majority of fans ran for cover, Dr. Fager continued in the driving rain, like some majestic shrouded figure. Sporting his usual figure-eight bridle, he wasted no time working up a bit of saliva. He focused straight ahead, arching his neck slightly, and his flared nostrils were already bright red. Through the deluge, Dr. Fager breezed his five furlongs in :59 under no pressure at all from Marrero.

As he left the track, the thunder still could be heard. But the lightning would not strike for another week. The Washington Park Handicap, run at Arlington Park, was the perfect vehicle for Dr. Fager to let it all out. This was where Baeza finally could step on the gas and just hold on. Everyone knew Buckpasser's world record, also set at Arlington, was in jeopardy. The only thing that could prevent Dr. Fager from breaking the record, other than the weather, was the 134 pounds racing secretary Larry Marsh piled on his back.

The only person who didn't seem to care about the record was Nerud. "Those things aren't important to me," he said. "I'm interested in winning, and you just try to handle a horse the best way you can to get him to win."

Dr. Fager arrived at Arlington two days before the race, right in the middle of an oppressive heat wave. As he had the previous year, he was on edge, and Nerud knew he had to watch him closely for fear of another colic attack. The afternoon before the race, Nerud sat with Dr. Fager and just talked to him and soothed him, trying to keep him settled. That night, Nerud walked him to keep him moving and help him relax. The horse eventually calmed down and was fine after that.

A cool wind whipped through the area on race day, breaking the sweltering heat and humidity. Nerud didn't give Baeza any specific instructions, and there was no talk of records. One look at Dr. Fager and he knew the colt was ready to do something big. If he was going to break the world record, he'd have to do it on his own. A field of ten was entered, and if there was any threat it likely would come from Racing Room, who was in receipt of eighteen pounds. In the span of one month, Racing Room had won the five and a half-furlong Hollywood Express Handicap in 1:02 2/5; finished third in the American Handicap on turf; finished second, beaten a neck, in the mile and a quarter Hollywood Gold Cup in 1:59 4/5; and won the mile and three-sixteenths Citation Handicap on turf.

Also in the field, carrying a feathery 112 pounds and going off at odds of nearly 48-1, was none other than Hedevar, who, ironically, was breaking right next to Dr. Fager. To further ensure a rapid pace was the three-year-old Kentucky Sherry, who had run the fastest opening six furlongs (1:09 4/5) and equaled the fastest opening half (:45 4/5) in the history of the Kentucky Derby earlier in the year.

Dr. Fager broke on top from post nine, but was taken in hand by Baeza, as Hedevar went whizzing by him on his outside to engage Kentucky Sherry and Angelico. Although all three looked as if they were in a Quarter Horse race, the opening quarter was run in a tame :22 4/5. Any thoughts of a world record looked dead and buried right there. Dr. Fager was still content to sit back in sixth, less than three lengths off the pace. As they continued down the backstretch, it was a mad scramble up front, as R. Thomas slipped through along the inside to stick his head in front. But Dr. Fager's red silks could be seen flying by horses on the far outside. The half-mile fraction on the tote board flashed :44. Dr. Fager had run his second quarter in an unheard of :20 3/5. It was believed to be the fastest quarter-mile fraction ever run in a non-sprint race and the fastest quarter within the body of a race at any distance.

Around the far turn, Dr. Fager began leaving the pack, with only Racing Room giving chase. Baeza kept the Doc well out from the rail and actually looked as if he were giving him a breather. It seemed as if the world's record was the furthest thing from his mind. Dr. Fager, as usual, had his head up and was cruising along, with Baeza turning for home about four paths off the rail. What the eye saw on the racetrack, however, was a stark contradiction from what flashed on the tote board. Dr. Fager had run his six furlongs in 1:07 3/5, with Baeza just sitting on him.

With a quarter of a mile to run, all he had to

do was shade :25 to break the record. But Baeza obviously had no idea how fast he was running or he would have given Dr. Fager a chance at it. Instead, he kept his hands motionless on the reins and let the big colt coast the rest of the way. Despite the lack of interest by his rider, Dr. Fager bounded away from the others on his own. Baeza could see nothing but that familiar long, black mane blowing wildly in his face. Inside the final furlong, the Doc's ears were straight up, and it was obvious there would be no last-ditch attempt at the record. The lead increased with each humongous stride. Dr. Fager crossed the wire eased up by ten lengths.

Track announcer Phil Georgeff, stunned by the performance, forgot to turn his microphone off. As Dr. Fager pulled up, out of the silence came a single, faint word: "Wow!"

Back then, it took about twenty-five seconds for the final time to be posted. After Dr. Fager finally was pulled up, Georgeff glanced back at the tote board and couldn't believe what he saw. He stepped back up to the mike and announced to the crowd, "Ladies and gentlemen, may we draw your attention to the final time of 1:32 1/5, which is a new world record!"

"He was just galloping through the stretch," Georgeff recalled, "and was running so effortlessly that I had forgotten all about the record, especially since he was carrying 134 pounds. When I saw the time I was shocked."

Baeza admitted he had no idea Dr. Fager was within reach of the record. "I never in any of his races knew how fast he was going," he said. "He moved so smoothly and his action was so fluid, I felt like I was in a Lear Jet. All I knew was that I was going faster than the rest of them. I'd try to slow him down, but he'd still pull away from them."

When Nerud saw his old jockey Ted Atkinson, who was now a state steward at Arlington, he told him, "Hell, he could have done it in thirty and change; he was six lengths within himself."

One person who would never forget this day was Dr. Fager's old friend from his youth, Al Roberts, who was serving in the Army Reserve at the time. Not only was Roberts able to rejoice in this news, but he also found out that same day his wife had given birth to a baby boy. "That made my son a real part of the horse," he said.

Dr. Fager's mark would become the most sought

after record in racing for the next thirty years. Based on his time, a study was made a year and a half later with the help of the St. Louis and Bronx Zoos, which concluded that Dr. Fager was faster than a cheetah, recognized as the fastest animal on Earth.

For Dr. Fager and Nerud, it was time for new worlds to conquer. Nerud nominated Dr. Fager to the mile and three-sixteenths United Nations Handicap, one of the most prestigious grass races in America, just to help Atlantic City Racetrack generate some publicity. Nerud had no intention of running. But with the timing right, coming eighteen days after the Washington Park Handicap, Nerud seriously began to consider the race. After thinking it over, he informed Atlantic City officials that Dr. Fager would run. "I thought, 'Hell, I'll send him down there and show them he can do anything,' " Nerud said. He knew a victory could give Dr. Fager an unprecedented four championships in a single year.

He had worked Dr. Fager on the grass nine days before the race and he seemed to handle it well, going a solid half in :48 4/5. He then shipped Dr. Fager to Atlantic City, where he breezed five furlongs in 1:02 over a soft course. The big colt didn't seem to handle the soft going that well, and Nerud could only hope the ground would be firm on race day. Although the turf was listed as firm, it was still wet and very slippery. Once again burdened with 134 pounds, Dr. Fager would have his work cut out for him.

To make matters even more difficult, the field assembled was one of the best in many years. Elliott Burch was confident Fort Marcy could upset Dr. Fager under the circumstances. Fort Marcy had already knocked off Damascus in the previous year's Washington, D.C., International, and he would be pulling sixteen pounds from Dr. Fager. Burch was convinced he had "everyone, including Dr. Fager, over a barrel at the weights."

Burch also had convinced himself that Dr. Fager would not handle the grass. "It's been my experience that speed horses on the dirt are usually not turf horses," he said. "They can't handle the turns. They tend to run out, and I think 'Fager' is going to have his problems keeping from racing wide."

Dr. Fager was stabled right next door to Tobin Bronze, the Australian "wonder horse," who had won twenty-four races Down Under, including a victory in the Caulfield Cup under 136 pounds. Like Fort Marcy, he was in the U.N. with 118. The day before, Tobin Bronze's trainer in Australia, Graham Heagney, who had come for the race, went over to Nerud and said, "I didn't think you'd come here." When Nerud asked him why, he replied, "Because there isn't a horse in the world who can give Tobin Bronze that much weight."

Dr. Fager also had to concede seventeen pounds to both Irish Rebellion, winner of the Pan American Handicap, and Flit-to, winner of the Seneca and Bougainvillea Handicaps; and twenty-two pounds to Advocator, who was more accomplished on the dirt, having won three major stakes, in addition to finishing second to In Reality in the Met Mile and second in the 1966 Kentucky Derby.

Dr. Fager, the 4-5 favorite, broke on top from post six, and Baeza went right to the front. But the challenge came quickly, as Laffit Pincay Jr. sent Advocator after him from the one hole. As Elliott Burch had predicted, Dr. Fager took the first turn very wide. Baeza could already sense he wasn't comfortable on the wet course. Around the clubhouse turn, Dr. Fager edged away to a length lead, with Advocator still dogging him, followed closely by Tobin Bronze. Down the backstretch, Pincay, one of the strongest riders in the country, began pumping his hands on Advocator and he slipped through along the inside to take command by a half-length.

Unlike the New Hampshire Sweepstakes when Dr. Fager tried to savage In Reality for attempting the same maneuver, the Doc had his mind on other matters, such as trying to grab hold of the slick turf. This time he offered little resistance to the challenge, and Baeza was quite content to let him sit back and try to find his best stride. "It was like he was ice skating," Baeza said. "He was slipping and sliding the whole way around. I kept pulling on him to get him to stick his head up and get a grip on the ground, but he just couldn't get hold of it. I was pretty worried, because he kept trying and trying and wasn't going anywhere."

Around the far turn, Baeza loosened up on the reins and Dr. Fager responded by charging up to challenge Advocator. Tobin Bronze was going nowhere behind them, but Fort Marcy was moving strongly along the hedge. At the quarter pole, Dr. Fager again went wide, while Advocator cut the corner and got his neck in front. It was obvious Dr. Fager was struggling. He had never lost the lead twice in one race, and conceding twenty-two pounds to a classy, hard-knocking horse, he looked in danger of being upset. But Dr. Fager dug in again and quickly stuck his head back in front as they passed the eighth pole.

Pincay reached back for all the strength he could muster. He began pushing hard with his left hand while pasting Advocator with a series of right-handed whips. To everyone's surprise, Advocator came back at Dr. Fager and opened nearly a half-length advantage approaching the sixteenth pole. Baeza, knowing the whip would only make matters worse, continued to hand ride Dr. Fager, who looked like a beaten horse. But this is where a true champion shines, and Dr. Fager wasn't through yet. With his blood at a boil, he pinned back his ears and went for it. Although there was no push to his legs, he took one final grab at the slick turf and thrust himself back in the lead. The tenacious Advocator still was relentless, but this time the Doc clenched his teeth and refused to let him come back. He crossed the wire a neck in front in the solid time of 1:55 1/5, with Fort Marcy closing well to be third. In some ways, this may have been Dr. Fager's greatest performance.

After the race McKnight turned to Nerud and said, "John, I've heard all my life about horses trying to win, and now I've seen it. I can't believe how he kept fighting and fighting."

Heagney also paid tribute to Dr. Fager. "If anyone had told me a horse could give Tobin Bronze that much weight and beat him I would have laughed in his face," he said. "But Dr. Fager is truly a great horse."

Advocator's trainer, Clyde Troutt, could only think out loud. "I wonder if my horse has any heart left?" he asked. "Though he still has four legs. All I can say is that the winner is one of the best horses I ever saw." Troutt would soon find out what Advocator was made of. In his next start, the Sunrise Handicap at Atlantic City, he broke the course record for a mile and a half. As for Fort Marcy, he would go on to be voted Horse of the Year two years later, and eventually inducted into the Hall of Fame.

Dr. Fager was a tired horse after the United Nations, and the Woodward Stakes in seventeen days came too soon. As it turned out, Damascus was upset in the Woodward by Mr. Right in a very slowly run race. It seemed obvious at that point that Damascus had seen his best days. His next race would be his last.

Nerud decided Dr. Fager had had enough distance races and wanted the horse to close out his career with a bang. He decided on the seven-furlong Vosburgh Handicap, but wanted it to be a special occasion, something the fans could remember for a long time. When Nerud told Trotter he was pointing for the Vosburgh, the racing secretary pondered how much weight to put on the horse. "I'll tell you how much to put on him, Tommy," he said. "I want you to put 145 on him, and then I'll send him home." But Trotter could not justify putting that much weight on any horse, especially picking up eleven pounds from his last start. It was a precedent in which he could not participate. As it was, he still raised Dr. Fager five pounds off the United Nations, assigning him a staggering 139 pounds.

This was the race in which Nerud would show off Dr. Fager. There were no more tomorrows. He had Dr. Fager primed for a big finale, and for the first time, he thought about breaking a record. But the day before the race, he noticed the track had changed dramatically. Hirsch Jacobs and his son John walked on the track that morning, and the elder Jacobs commented, "It's pretty deep today." The surface had been winterized, putting in a deeper cushion that made the track considerably slower.

Dr. Fager's main threat in the Vosburgh looked to be Kissin' George. The California speedster had been sent East and turned over to Allen Jerkens after winning the six-furlong Peninsula Handicap at Bay Meadows in 1:08 4/5 under 128 pounds. In his first start for Jerkens, he won the Sport Page Handicap at Belmont by three and a half lengths in 1:09 1/5, the fastest six furlongs of the meet.

Kissin' George was assigned 127 pounds for the Vosburgh, followed by the hard-hitting Jim J. at 125. The low weight at 105 was a horse named Villamor, who would be in receipt of an unheard of thirty-four pounds from Dr. Fager.

The night before the race, Dr. Fager started acting a little colicky, so Nerud stayed with him until two o'clock in the morning, walking him and giving him baking soda to help settle his stomach. He couldn't treat the horse with medication, because it was too close to the race and he would have risked a positive drug test. In his forty-seven years as a trainer, Nerud never was fined or suspended. Dr. Fager came out of it fine, and was none the worse for wear on race day.

Dr. Fager broke from post three, with Kissin' George coming out of the six-hole. This was an opportunity for Kissin' George to get the jump on Dr. Fager, who had been running in distance races all year. The last time they had met, in the Californian, Kissin' George outran Dr. Fager for five furlongs, and gave him quite a tussle around the far turn. As he did then, he burst out of the gate on top, but Baeza quickly had Dr. Fager eyeball to eyeball with him on the inside. After an opening quarter in :22 1/5, both horses were at each other's throat. Bill Boland was all over Kissin' George, pushing and scrubbing, but he couldn't shake loose from Dr. Fager.

Still locked together, they blazed the half in a spectacular :43 4/5. But it was a familiar scenario, with one horse in an all-out drive and Dr. Fager cruising alongside, just humoring him. Turning for home, Baeza let the big horse loose and he kissed Kissin' George good-bye. "He went by me at the three-sixteenths pole like I was tied," Boland said. "And my horse was running pretty good at that point."

As he did in the Washington Park Handicap, Dr. Fager drew clear under no urging at all from Baeza. He led by three lengths at the eighth pole, as the crowd began its thunderous salute to a great champion. Despite the slower winterized track and 139 pounds on his back, Dr. Fager had scorched the six furlongs in 1:07 4/5, four-fifths of a second faster than Near Man's track record for the distance, set in 1963 under 112 pounds.

Dr. Fager continued to pour it on, with Baeza merely hand riding him. He crossed the wire six lengths ahead of Kissin' George. His time of 1:20 1/5 broke Rose Net's track record by a full second and came within a fifth of a second of the world record.

"John said this was his last hurrah, let him put on a show," Baeza said. "I was concerned about the 139 pounds, but at the quarter pole I was already looking back. There was no competition, so I took a hold of him. If I knew how fast he was going, I would have chirped to him and he likely would have gone faster. It was like a Rolls Royce up against Volkswagens."

Boland came back and was in awe of the horse he had ridden in the previous year's Woodward Stakes. "I don't know if he was all out at the finish, but when he was close enough for me to judge, Baeza had him under a tight hold. I couldn't believe it."

And Nerud still talked about the track. "I can't imagine how fast he would have run if they had pulled some of that cushion off and got the track back to where it was fast," Nerud said. "He would have smoked a little, wouldn't he?"

*New York Post* racing columnist William Rudy, writing in *The Thoroughbred Record*, opened his story by saying, "Dr. Fager said goodbye with one of the great performances in New York racing history."

It was a fitting conclusion to what many believe to be the single greatest campaign ever. The Doc had his four championships, including Horse of the Year, and records that would endure for decades. He retired with eighteen victories in twenty-two starts, although he finished first nineteen times. It took a rabbit, the stewards, and a bad ride to beat him. In eight starts at four, his average weight carried was over 133 pounds. Only three horses ever finished in front of him, and two of them were inducted into the Hall of Fame.

Although he only faced Damascus four times, their rivalry was one of the most heated in the history of the sport, and each horse helped define the other's greatness.

"Damascus was a damn good horse," Nerud said. "I eventually bred to him and got Ogygian. The fans loved the rivalry. People think there was animosity between Whiteley and me, but we never got mad at each other. We just did what we had to and never asked where the other one was going to run. Frank was a pretty decent guy. I know I can be abrupt and blurt out things I probably shouldn't, but it's the goddamn truth. When you tell the truth, you're an oddball."

There have been many superlatives used to describe Dr. Fager, but in the end it all seems to come down to one. After the Vosburgh, Bill Boland, still shaking his head in disbelief, tried to find the right word to portray the beast who had just devoured his brilliant horse. He hesitated only for a second, then said, "A freak, that's what he is."

# Memory Of The Wind

John Nerud ran all aspects of the Tartan operation with the same iron-handed approach he did everything else in his life. But he knew there was one thing he had no control over. When Dr. Fager departed Belmont Park on that November morning, not only did Nerud feel empty, he felt helpless. No one knew the horse like he and Dimitrijevic did, and neither of them would be there any longer to keep a close eye on him and get him through the rough times, as they had so often in the past three years.

All Nerud could do was forewarn farm manager John Hartigan. "The first time this horse has colic you're gonna lose him unless you do what I tell you," he said. "You give him double the relaxant you'd give a normal horse. If that doesn't work, you give him another double dose."

No one really had any idea what kind of sire Dr. Fager would make. Although he was regarded as one of the fastest horses, if not the fastest, who ever lived, there was plenty in his pedigree to suggest he could produce a horse to stay classic distances, just as he did. Aspidistra, although a mediocre race-horse at best, still was bred by the powerful King Ranch. In her pedigree were names like Man o' War, Better Self, Black Toney, Bimelech, Bull Dog, and War Admiral. In her third generation was the blue hen producer La Troienne, and she was inbred 4x4 to the great foundation stallion Teddy. What Nerud loved about her was that she traced to Domino twice through Peter Pan, sire of Black Toney. Years later, Nerud would also look to the Domino line to get Fappiano, who raced in his name and would become one of the nation's most dominant sires.

In August of his four-year-old campaign, Dr. Fager was syndicated, with McKnight retaining twelve shares and Nerud keeping four. Five shares were sold for $100,000 per share, while eleven other individuals bought seasons under a four-year contract for $10,000 per service, with no guaran-tee of live foal. Based on the figures, Dr. Fager's syndicate value was listed at $3.2 million, making him the third highest syndicated stallion of all time behind Vaguely Noble and Buckpasser. Four months later, his arch rival Damascus was syndicated for $2,560,000.

Because he was a complete outcross, he attracted the attention of some of the nation's leading breeders. Bull Hancock, owner of Claiborne Farm, tried hard to get Dr. Fager. He told Nerud, "John, he's the perfect horse. I can breed him to anything." But Nerud had no intentions of parting with Dr. Fager. In him, he saw the future of Tartan Farm, and in many ways, the future of the Florida breeding industry.

Dr. Fager's professionalism carried over to the breeding shed. By the time he arrived at the farm, Al Roberts was in charge of the stallions, enabling him to rekindle the friendship that had begun the day the horse was born. Roberts eventually would take over as co-manager of the farm along with Bryan Howlett after Hartigan left in 1976. "Dr. Fager hadn't changed much in the three years he was away," Roberts said. "He still was a great horse in everything he did. And even as a stud, one thing about him that never changed was that you could still hurt his feelings if you scolded him.

He could be breeding a mare, and if things weren't going right and you yelled, 'Down Fager,' he would jump down in a second like he knew something was wrong. We would put him in the wash rack to clean him up after breeding, and he was so good I could just pull the shank up and hang it on his ear as we were washing him."

Dr. Fager also was reunited at Tartan Farm with an old antagonist, In Reality, who like Dr. Fager and Damascus would become one of the top sires in the country. "In Reality was directly across the shed from Dr. Fager," Roberts said. "He was like a little bulldog, and we used to call him 'War Bonnet.' He was always fired up. He'd get up on his hind legs and was raring to go. Dr. Fager was more of a lover. He'd get up on a mare and would just like to rub on them."

While Dr. Fager was adapting to his new life, back at the racetrack his kid half-sister Ta Wee, by Intentionally, was building up quite a reputation of her own. Unlike her brother, Ta Wee was strictly a sprinter, but what a sprinter she was. After knocking off the boys as a three-year-old in the 1969 Fall Highweight Handicap under 130 pounds, and the Vosburgh Handicap, she succeeded her brother as champion sprinter. The following year, she emulated Dr. Fager with feats of weight carrying not seen before by a filly. She captured five of her seven starts, winning the Correction Handicap under 131 pounds, the Hempstead with 132, and the Regret carrying 136. Facing the top male sprinters in the country, she demonstrated the tenacity of her half-brother, winning the Fall Highweight under a staggering 140 pounds. In her career finale, she had little trouble in the Interborough Handicap, winning in hand carrying an unprecedented 142 pounds. In her only defeat of the summer, she was beaten by the classy sprinter Distinctive in the Gravesend Handicap, carrying 134 pounds and conceding twenty pounds to the winner.

Named champion sprinter for the second consecutive year, Ta Wee was retired to Tartan Farm in the fall of 1970. As she was led off the van by Fred Dimitrijevic, awaiting her at the bottom of the ramp was her mother Aspidistra and Dr. Fager. Ta Wee stopped at the top of the ramp to pose for a memorable family photo that made its way into numerous publications.

Dr. Fager's first few years at stud were not as productive as everyone had hoped. By the end of 1973, his first two crops produced only one restricted stakes winner, Plastic Surgeon, winner of the Rosemont Stakes at Delaware Park. Nerud decided to lower his stud fee from $25,000 to $20,000. But he still had faith that, given time, Dr. Fager would become a top sire.

"I wasn't discouraged," he said. "If you go back through history, you'll find that when a horse is retired at four, it usually takes him eight years to hit his peak. I always felt, because Dr. Fager was such a big, strapping horse and was by Rough'n Tumble, a sire of colts, that he would be a sire of colts as well. But his best horses were fillies."

In June of 1974, Dr. Fager's fortunes suddenly changed. In the span of six days, Tree of Knowledge won the mile and a quarter Hollywood Gold Cup, Lady Love captured the Molly Pitcher Handicap at Monmouth, and Lie Low won the Open Fire Stakes at Delaware Park. Dr. Fager finally had broken through. At the end of the year he was the ninth-leading sire in the country. Although many felt, because of his awesome speed, he would produce precocious youngsters, the opposite was true. Dr. Fager's progeny took their time to develop and didn't reach their peak until three and four.

Ironically, it was Damascus who would wind up siring brilliant two-year-olds.

Dr. Fager continued to turn out top-class horses of all ages. They could win sprinting or going a distance, on dirt or turf. In 1975, he produced the two-year-old filly champion Dearly Precious, who won eight of her nine starts, including the Spinaway, Arlington-Washington Lassie, and Sorority Stakes. In all, she won seven consecutive stakes, and twice defeated Optimistic Gal, who won five major stakes that year by an average margin of eight and a half lengths. Dearly Precious helped Dr. Fager catapult to third on the 1975 leading sires list, with earnings of more than $1.2 million.

Dearly Precious' three-year-old campaign was cut short by injury, but not before she had won the Acorn Stakes, defeating Optimistic Gal again, as well as the Dark Mirage, Prioress, and Flirtation Stakes.

Times were good at Tartan Farm, and as the 1976 breeding season came to an end, everyone looked ahead to another long, hot Ocala summer. The evening of August 5 seemed just like any other. Roberts, who alternated night duty with Howlett, was on call that particular evening. All seemed normal, as the night watchman went through his evening rounds. He looked in on Dr. Fager, who was standing quietly in his stall.

His next time around, however, he noticed something was wrong with the big horse and quickly called Roberts. After arriving at the stallion barn, Roberts could see that Dr. Fager was beginning to show signs of colic. He had come down with colic several times while at the farm, but would always come through in about thirty minutes with normal treatment.

It was now approaching nine o'clock and Roberts called veterinarian Dr. Ruben Brawner on his car phone. Brawner had just finished visiting his wife in the hospital and was on his way home when he got the call from Roberts. When Brawner arrived at the farm, Dr. Fager was in distress. He had him brought into the breeding shed where there was more room to work, and treated him in the usual manner. Through a stomach tube, he gave the horse a gallon of mineral oil to act as a laxative. Mixed in with the mineral oil was a normal dose of chloral hydrate, which acted as a sedative and pain killer, and a normal dose of Tercapsol, an anti-ferment to help prevent gas from forming. He also injected him with a dose of the muscle relaxant diperone hydrochloride.

A half-hour later, Dr. Fager showed no sign of improvement, so Brawner gave him another dose of all the medications and injected him with fluids intravenously. But once again, it did little good. Brawner could see this was no ordinary case of colic. He knew something was dreadfully wrong. By now Dr. Fager was sweating and trembling and in terrible pain. His pulse had soared to more than 100. Brawner called Dr. William Lyle, who had a surgery nearby. Lyle came with his associate, Dr. Chip Estes, and continued to work on the horse, with no results. Then a fourth vet, Dr. Ronald Chak, arrived to offer his assistance. They placed a trocar, a sharp instrument with an attached tube, through the horse's flank and into his intestine in an attempt to allow the gas to escape.

It was now past eleven, and all four veterinarians came to the same realization. They were going to lose him. Surgery, which was not very common back then, was out of the question. The horse had deteriorated so quickly and was thrashing about so wildly it was impossible to move him. He was now swelling up and getting tighter and tighter. Roberts contacted the insurance company, who sent a representative to the farm. At 11:30 p.m., Dr. Fager's suffering was over. The mighty warrior, for the first time in his life, had no fight left in him, and he lay down and died.

Just like that, the great Dr. Fager was gone. The almost-mystical fire that had set the Sport of Kings ablaze for three years was extinguished forever. Because of the insurance, an autopsy was performed in the stallion barn. It was discovered that Dr. Fager had died of a ruptured stomach. "Even with all of today's modern techniques, we still wouldn't have been able to save him," Brawner said. "It was hard seeing him go like that. I'll never forget what a tough, great big beautiful animal he was; one of the most beautiful I ever saw."

"He fought so hard," Roberts said. "It was only about two hours from his first symptom of colic to the time he died. He was such an athlete and such a fighter, he never showed any signs of pain. He died like a true racehorse."

It was Roberts' unpleasant task to call Nerud in Saratoga and break the news to him. "I sure didn't look forward to that," he said. "I felt like I had lost a member of my family. It's just a shame he had to be taken from our midst so early. I had to get my emotions out, so I wrote an article about him for the Tartan newspaper."

The following morning, blacksmiths John Pendray and his son Alfred were driving into the farm and their hearts sunk at the sight off to their right. Both had worked with Dr. Fager since he was a foal. When they saw a horse being placed in a newly dug grave, John Pendray gasped, "Oh no! Don't tell me." He turned to his son and said, "I don't like what I'm seeing." They drove to the barn and were told the tragic news.

Karina Dimitrijevic, daughter of assistant trainer Joe Dimitrijevic, remembers her parents breaking the news to her. Twelve at the time, she had been born the same year as Dr. Fager, and her parents would bring her to the barn often. Her mother worked as a secretary and bookkeeper for Nerud. As a child, she can remember going to the barn and all the excitement over this one big, special horse. "I can remember the look of shock on their faces when they came home that next morning and told me Dr. Fager had died," she said. "They knew how special he was to me."

As fate would have it, the next year Dr. Fager was the leading sire in the country with earnings of almost $1.6 million. He had become only the fourth stallion based outside of Kentucky to top the sires list in this century. In 1978, his son, Dr. Patches, upset Triple Crown winner Seattle Slew in the Paterson Handicap on his way to being named co-champion sprinter. His other major victories came in the seven-furlong Vosburgh and mile and a quarter Meadowlands Cup, a fitting tribute to the versatility of his sire. That year, Dr. Fager was the nation's second leading sire.

Dr. Fager would go on to leave a lasting legacy, especially through his daughters. Through 1999, he is the broodmare sire of 98 stakes winners and 55 stakes-placed horses. His influence was felt as recently as the '99 Breeders' Cup, where his granddaughter Shared Interest, winner of the grade I Ruffian Handicap, was represented by two runners: Cash Run, who captured the Juvenile Fillies, and grade I winner Forestry, who finished fourth in the Sprint. Dr. Fager also is the broodmare sire of Maudlin, whose daughter Beautiful Pleasure clinched the older filly and mare title by winning the Distaff. Most fittingly, Dr. Fager is the sire of the second dam of Artax, who won the Sprint in track record-equaling time and was named champion sprinter.

One of the most uniquely bred horses of recent times was Fappiano's son Quiet American, who is inbred 3x2 to Dr. Fager. Winner of the grade I NYRA Mile, he would sire Kentucky Derby and Preakness winner Real Quiet, following in the footsteps of Fappiano, who sired Kentucky Derby and Breeders' Cup Classic winner Unbridled. As a broodmare sire, Dr. Fager also produced major stakes winners Cure the Blues, Sewickley, Too Chic, Coup de Fusil, Leroy S., and the grade I-winning turf stars Equalize, Great Neck, and Tantalizing.

In 1978, William McKnight died, and his daughter, Mrs. James Binger, took over the Tartan operation. But she had little interest in the horses and turned control over to her husband. Two years later, Tartan would win its first classic when Codex, trained by a relatively unknown former Quarter Horse trainer named D. Wayne Lukas, captured the Preakness Stakes. It was Nerud, now concentrating more on the breeding and managerial end of the operation, who discovered Lukas' talents and gave him his first break.

In addition to Fappiano, Nerud also would breed Cozzene, who raced in his colors and was trained by his son Jan. Cozzene would win the Breeders' Cup Mile, be named champion turf male, and sire Breeders' Cup Classic winner Alphabet Soup and Breeders' Cup Turf winner Tikkanen. With Jan as trainer, Tartan went on to win major stakes with Acaroid, Great Neck, Who's for Dinner, and Ogygian. On the West Coast, Lukas took the Santa Anita Derby with Muttering. Nerud also bred Unbridled for Tartan, but the colt was sold at auction as a weanling when Binger announced in June of 1987 he was dispersing nearly all of Tartan's Thoroughbred holdings, due to increasing costs and low profits.

By the early '90s, the empire that McKnight and Nerud built from nothing had been reduced to a lifeless tract of land. The fields which once were the playground for racing's greatest horses were now home to three aging broodmares and an old gelding who was living out his final days. The farm eventually was purchased by breeder Harry T. Mangurian Jr. to add on to his adjacent Mockingbird Farm.

Although Tartan Farm is gone, there is one section of hallowed ground that has remained untouched. Atop a hill, overlooking the serenity of Lake Ta Wee is the old cemetery. There, behind a cedar tree and shaded by two oak trees are the headstones of those who helped build the Tartan dynasty. Bryan Howlett still goes up there now and then, just to walk around and remember the way it was. They're all there — Aspidistra, Ta Wee, Cequillo, Intentionally, My Dear Girl, Codex, and others.

But there is one that still shouts out after all these years, echoing through the breezes that blow into the valley below. Beneath the headstone of Dr. Fager, Howlett placed a flat piece of granite, on which is inscribed: "Racing's Grand Slam...1968 Horse of the Year, Handicap Champion, Sprint Champion, Grass Champion...Set World Record for a Mile." As you read the inscription, images of the mighty Dr. Fager flash across the landscape that had once been his home. Even after three decades, you can still see that long mane blowing wildly in the breeze. You can see the fire raging in his eyes. You can feel the spirit of this unharnessed force of nature. And you too remember. Perhaps the late racing writer David Alexander said it best: "The memory of him is the memory of the wind. I shall remember the brilliant Dr. Fager like a sudden shaft of sunlight on a darkening day."

# Pedigree

| | | Questionnaire, 1927 | Sting |
| | | | Miss Puzzle |
| | Free For All, 1942 | | |
| | | Panay, 1934 | Chicle |
| | | | Panasette |
| ROUGH'N TUMBLE, | | | |
| b, 1948 | | | |
| | | **Bull Dog**, 1927 | Teddy |
| | | | Plucky Liege |
| | Roused, 1943 | | |
| | | Rude Awakening, | Upset |
| | | 1936 | Cushion |
| **DR. FAGER,** | | | |
| **b h,** | | | |
| **April 6, 1964** | | | |
| | | Bimelech, 1937 | Black Toney |
| | | | La Troienne |
| | Better Self, 1945 | | |
| | | Bee Mac, 1941 | War Admiral |
| | | | Baba Kenny |
| ASPIDISTRA, | | | |
| b, 1954 | | | |
| | | Bull Brier, 1938 | **Bull Dog** |
| | | | Rose Eternal |
| | Tilly Rose, 1948 | | |
| | | Tilly Kate, 1935 | Draymont |
| | | | Teak |

# DR. FAGER'S RACE RECORD

**Dr. Fager** — **b. c. 1964, by Rough'n Tumble (Free for All)–Aspidistra, by Better Self** — **Lifetime record: 22 18 2 1 $1,002,642**

**Own.– Tartan Stable**
**Br.– Tartan Farms (Fla)**
**Tr.– John A. Nerud**

| Date/Race | Cond. | Dist. | Fractions | Race | PP | St | 1st | 2nd | Str | Fin | Jockey | Wt | Odds | Figs | Top finishers | Comment | Field |
|---|---|---|---|---|---|---|---|---|---|---|---|---|---|---|---|---|---|
| 2Nov68- 7Aqu | fst | 7f | :221 :434 1:074 1:201 3↑ | Vosburgh H 57k | 3 | 4 | 1hd | 1hd | 13 | 16 | Baeza B | 139 | *.30 | 105–12 | Dr.Fager1396Kissin'George1276JmJ.125hd | Under mild drive | 7 |
| 11Sep68- 8Atl | fm | 1 3/16 (T) | :484 1:123 1:364 1:551 3↑ | U Nations H 100k | 6 | 1 | 1hd | 2hd | 1hd | 1nk | Baeza B | 134 | *.80 | 94–10 | Dr.Fgr134nkAdvoctor1121¼FortMrcy1181¼ | Under stiff drive | 9 |
| 24Aug68- 8AP | fst | 1 | :224 :44 1:073 1:321 3↑ | Washington Park H 112k | 9 | 6 | 2hd | 1½ | 13 | 110 | Baeza B | 134 | *.30 | 102–10 | Dr. Fager13410Racing Room1161½Info1121 | Easily best | 10 |
| 3Aug68- 6Sar | fst | 1⅛ | :471 1:113 1:363 1:484 3↑ | Whitney 53k | 2 | 1 | 1½ | 13 | 13 | 18 | Baeza B | 132 | *.05 | 97–12 | Dr. Fager1328Spoon Bait1141Fort Drum11415 | Much the best | 4 |
| 20Jly68- 7Aqu | fst | 1¼ | :454 1:092 1:343 1:591 3↑ | Brooklyn H 109k | 3 | 2 | 21½ | 1½ | 2½ | 22½ | Baeza B | 135 | *.60 | 99–13 | Damascus1302½Dr.Fager1353Mr.Right114hd | Rank early going | 7 |
| 4Jly68- 7Aqu | fst | 1¼ | :482 1:11 1:343 1:593 3↑ | Suburban H 107k | 3 | 1 | 1½ | 1hd | 12 | 12 | Baeza B | 132 | *.80 | 100–11 | Dr.Fager1322BoldHour1163Damascus1333½ | Under mild drive | 5 |
| 18May68- 8Hol | fst | 1 1/16 | :222 :45 1:083 1:404 3↑ | Californian 119k | 11 | 4 | 2½ | 1½ | 14 | 13 | Baeza B | 130 | *1.20 | 91–13 | Dr. Fager1303Gamely1161Rising Market1211½ | Much the best | 14 |
| 4May68- 7Aqu | fst | 7f | :222 :45 1:084 1:212 3↑ | Roseben H 54k | 5 | 1 | 1½ | 11 | 13 | 13 | Rotz JL | 130 | *.20 | 99–17 | Dr. Fager1303Tumiga1213Diplomat Way121¾ | Won eased up | 5 |
| 7Nov67- 7Aqu | fst | 7f | :222 :451 1:093 1:213 3↑ | Vosburgh H 57k | 6 | 8 | 52½ | 2hd | 1hd | 14½ | Baeza B | 128 | *.20e | 98–16 | Dr. Fager1284½Jim J.1151½R. Thomas1223 | Wide,easily best | 9 |
| 21Oct67- 8Haw | fst | 1¼ | :461 1:101 1:351 2:011 3↑ | Haw Gold Cup H 121k | 1 | 1 | 1½ | 1hd | 11½ | 12½ | Baeza B | 123 | *.30 | 90–12 | Dr.Fager1232½WhisperJt1141¼Pontmnow1081¼ | Without urging | 7 |
| 30Sep67- 7Aqu | fst | 1¼ | :451 1:091 1:353 2:003 3↑ | Woodward 107k | 2 | 1 | 1hd | 2½ | 25 | 310½ | Boland W | 120 | 1.80 | 84–15 | Damascus12010Buckpasser126½Dr. Fager12013 | Faltered | 6 |
| 2Sep67- 8Rkm | fst | 1¼ | :463 1:11 1:351 1:594 | NH Sweep Classic 265k | 1 | 1 | 1½ | 2hd | 2hd | 11¼ | Baeza B | 120 | *.20 | 115–17 | Dr.Fager1201¼InReality1269BarbsDelight1152¾ | Mild drive | 5 |
| 15Jly67- 9Rkm | fst | 1⅛ | :462 1:101 1:353 1:481 | Rkm Spl 85k | 5 | 1 | 16½ | 13½ | 13½ | 14¼ | Baeza B | 124 | *.10 | 105–15 | Dr.Fager1244¼ReasontoHail1214¾JackofAllTrds1128¼ | Easily | 7 |
| 24Jun67- 8AP | sly | 1 | :224 :45 1:102 1:36 | AP Classic 106k | 1 | 3 | 3nk | 13 | 16 | 110 | Baeza B | 120 | *.40 | 83–25 | Dr.Fager12010LightningOrphan1161¾DiplomatWay1187 | Easily | 6 |
| 30May67- 7GS | fst | 1⅛ | :47 1:103 1:353 1:48 | Jersey Derby 119k | 4 | 1 | 1½ | 12 | 13 | 16½ | Ycaza M | 126 | *.30 | 97–14 | [D]Dr.Fager1266½InReality1268AirRghts12612 | Crowded field | 4 |
| Disqualified and placed fourth | | | | | | | | | | | | | | | | | |
| 13May67- 7Aqu | fst | 1 | :223 :441 1:08 1:334 | Withers 58k | 8 | 4 | 21 | 2hd | 11½ | 16 | Baeza B | 126 | *.80 | 99–16 | Dr. Fager1266Tumiga1265Reason to Hail1265 | Easy score | 8 |
| 15Apr67- 7Aqu | fst | 1 | :233 :461 1:102 1:351 | Gotham 57k | 5 | 4 | 33 | 3nk | 2hd | 1½ | Ycaza M | 122 | *1.30e | 92–14 | Dr. Fager122½Damascus1225Reason to Hail1147 | Driving | 9 |
| 15Oct66- 7Aqu | fst | 1 | :222 :444 1:092 1:35 | Champagne 208k | 7 | 4 | 3½ | 1hd | 13 | 21 | Shoemaker W | 122 | *1.00 | 92–14 | Successor1221Dr. Fager1224Proviso1224 | Rank early,failed | 10 |
| 5Oct66- 7Aqu | gd | 7f | :224 :46 1:113 1:244 | Cowdin 88k | 1 | 10 | 31 | 32 | 21½ | 1¾ | Shoemaker W | 117 | *.80 | 82–22 | Dr.Fager117¾InRlty1171½Succssor1172½ | Slow start,driving | 10 |
| 10Sep66- 8Atl | fst | 7f | :223 :452 1:103 1:231 | World's Playground 28k | 3 | 6 | 1hd | 1½ | 14 | 112 | Ycaza M | 115 | *.90 | 87–24 | Dr. Fager11512Glengary1153½Pointsman115hd | Much the best | 11 |
| 13Aug66- 4Sar | fst | 6f | :223 :462 1:102 | Alw 5500 | 5 | 5 | 21½ | 22 | 12 | 18 | Hidalgo D5 | 117 | *.90 | 96–09 | Dr. Fager1178Bandera Road1172Quaker City1152 | Easily | 8 |
| 15Jly66- 3Aqu | fst | 5½f | :224 :464 :59 1:05 | ©Md Sp Wt | 8 | 8 | 83 | 21 | 11½ | 17 | Hidalgo D5 | 117 | 10.80 | 88–20 | Dr. Fager1177Lift Off1224Rising Market122½ | Easily best | 11 |

Past Performances courtesy Daily Racing Form LLC © 1999, reprinted from the book "Champions" (DRF Press)

# Index

# Photo Credits

*Cover photo:* (Bob Coglianese)

Page 1: Aspidistra (Arthur Kunkel); Rough'n Tumble (The Blood-Horse); Better Self (New York Racing Association Photo); Dr. Fager (Jim Jernigan)

Page 2: Tartan Farm yearlings (Jim Jernigan); Tartan yearling barn (Art Kunkel); Tartan Farm aerial (Art Kunkel)

Page 3: Dr. Fager winning the Cowdin (Mike Sirico); Dr. Fager and John Nerud (The Blood-Horse); David Hidalgo, W. L. McKnight, John Nerud (Leo Frutkoff)

Page 4: John Nerud and James Binger (Kerry Heubeck); Bill Shoemaker (The Blood-Horse); Manuel Ycaza (Bob Coglianese); Braulio Baeza (Winants Bros.); Dr. Fager (The Blood-Horse)

Page 5: Dr. Fager winning the Gotham (Mike Sirico); Dr. Fager's public workout (Bob Coglianese); Dr. Fager works (Paul Schafer)

Page 6: After winning the Withers (Bob Coglianese); Jersey Derby (Turfotos)

Page 7: Dr. Fager winning the Arlington Classic (The Blood-Horse); Working in front of renovated Belmont Park (The Blood-Horse); Morning routine (The Blood-Horse)

Page 8: Dr. Fager getting toweled off; Standing with Spasoje Dimitrijevic, et al.; Working with Jose Marrero up (all courtesy of Fred Dimitrijevic)

Page 9: Dr. Fager walking down to saddling area; in post parade (both courtesy of Fred Dimitrijevic); Dr. Fager winning the Suburban (Bob Coglianese); Damascus winning the Brooklyn (Mike Sirico)

Page 10-11: Dr. Fager's world-record mile (The Blood-Horse); Dr. Fager with Jose Marrero up (Paul Schafer); Winning the Whitney (Bob Coglianese)

Page 12: Dr. Fager being sculpted (Paul Schafer); Winning the Vosburgh (Bob Coglianese); Winning the United Nations (Turfotos)

Page 13: Dr. Fager leaving Belmont Park (Paul Schafer); Getting a speeding "citation" (Courtesy of The Florida Horse)

Page 14: Dr. Fager in his paddock (Jim Jernigan); Ta Wee arrives (Arthur Kunkel); Dr. Fager in 1974 (Jim Jernigan)

Page 15: Dr. Patches (Bob Coglianese); Unbridled (Skip Dickstein); Dearly Precious (Turfotos)

Page 16: Dr. Fager (Arthur Kunkel); Farm sign and gravestone (Barbara D. Livingston)

# Steve Haskin

S teve Haskin, is an award-winning turf writer and national correspondent for *The Blood-Horse*, the leading Thoroughbred industry weekly. Haskin spent twenty-nine years with *Daily Racing Form*, and became known for his insightful coverage of the Triple Crown races. Haskin won the Red Smith Award for best Kentucky Derby advance and the David Woods Award for best Preakness story in 1997.

In 1999, he co-authored Baffert: *Dirt Road to the Derby* with trainer Bob Baffert. Haskin has written for many publications, including *The Thoroughbred Record, The Backstretch, Pacemaker International, The British Racehorse, Louisiana Horse, Stud & Stable*, and *The Sporting Chronicle*. He has also provided research for many book projects as well as to ABC-TV. He lives in Hamilton Square, New Jersey with his wife and daughter.